A Self Help Book
How To
Achieve Just About Anything

Book License Notes

Reference

The materials contained in this book are guidelines to self-improvement through merit.

As an engineer and CEO, I found dramatic parallels between the pursuit of perfection in manufacturing and being able to improve one's personal position in the world.

Cover Art

Extraordinary Cover Illustrations are provided by Renowned Minnesota Graphic Illustrator M C Henry.

Table of Contents

Merit

**Obtaining
Uncommon Sense**

The benefits of succeeding through Merit

When I think of MERIT these words come to mind.
Achievement, Trust, integrity, worthy, value, esteem, deserve, praise, class, excellence, earn, recognition, appreciation, virtue, dignity, just, credit, reward and so on.

What merit isn't.
Disadvantage, Disrespect, Ill Repute, Worthlessness, Dishonor, Evil, Wickedness, Detriment, Weakness, Hate, jealousy, revenge, distain, having a grudge, getting even, political, religious, racist, destroying others, creating a crisis, canceling a culture, making certain your opponent loses.

Perceive or perception. Same Difference.

Webster Says

merit

noun

mer·it | \ ˈmer-ət, ˈme-rət \

Definition of *merit*

(Entry 1 of 2)

1a: a praiseworthy quality : VIRTUE But originality, as it is one of the highest, is also one of the rarest, of *merits*.— Edgar Allan Poe

b: character or conduct deserving reward, honor, or esteem *also* : ACHIEVEMENT… he composed a number of works of *merit*.— H. E. Starr

c: the qualities or actions that constitute the basis of one's deserts Opinions of his *merit* vary.

D *obsolete:* reward or punishment due

2a merits *plural*: the substance of a legal case apart from matters of jurisdiction, procedure, or form the plaintiff … is entitled to have its claim decided here on its *merits*. — T. M. Maddes

b: individual significance or justification (see JUSTIFICATION SENSE 1)The contention is without *merit*.— E. B. Denny

3: spiritual credit held to be earned by performance of righteous acts and to ensure future benefits.,. the Crusades … did serve the desire to gain spiritual *merit* …—
Jacques Barzun

merit

verb

merited; **meriting**; **merits**
Definition of *merit* **(Entry 2 of 2)**
transitive verb
: to be worthy of or entitled or liable
to **:** EARN
intransitive verb
1: DESERVE
2: *obsolete:* to be entitled to reward or honor

Something deserving reward, praise, or gratitude.
noun
A reward or honor given for superior qualities or conduct; mark, badge, etc. awarded for excellence.
noun
Intrinsic rightness or wrongness apart from formalities, emotional considerations, etc.

Marines are taught to be able to overcome any obstacle, which serves them well in the uncertainties and confusion of combat. This concept is encapsulated in the Marine slogan "Improvise, Adapt, and Overcome". This concept is a mindset that allows Marines to deal with any physical, mental, or spiritual hardship.

Common Sense

Common sense is subjective. Your common sense is what got you where you are today. This book was put together to change that. Not to take your common sense away, but to enhance your perception of common sense and build on that foundation. Hopefully following regiments laid out in this book will give you, "Uncommon Sense".

You know what your problem is - you have too much free time.

Free time is important and every-one needs time to kick back and relax. Analyze how you spend your free time. Managing your time can benefit you tremendously. Method described later.

Release Your Potential

Deep within all of us lies a greater self. Through the process of elimination, we can systematically shed bad habits and replace them with good ones.

Three Steps to Success with Merit

Achievement; a thing done successfully, typically by effort, courage, or skill.
Accomplishment; Something that has been achieved successfully. An activity that a person can do well, typically as a result of study and or practice.
Acknowledgment; An acceptance of the truth or existence of something. To recognize the fact or importance or quality of.

"I never dreamed about success, I worked for it."
-- Estee Lauder

Merit Since the Beginning

The presents of merit are infinitely evident in nature. Out of the primordial ooze, even microbes were dependent on merit.

Single celled organisms appeared on earth approximately 3.5 billion years ago. The slow evolution into more intricate multicellular animals didn't occur until around 600 million years ago.

Multicellular entities benefited from surrounding themselves with like living structures. They mutated into relying on each other. Their propensity to break free of this coexistence was inevitably curbed by survival. Yet they were always only one mutation away from being intrinsically independent.

As time went on mutations would create totally unique individual entities thriving on one another's intermingling. The hierarchy in these living entities have been totally dependent on merit. What one does for the other and so on.

Eventually substructures began to shirk the responsibilities others around them provided and they would grow their dependence and lose their ability to survive on their own.

Plants and animals fight for their existence in the world and those that survive do it through MERIT.

Plants fight for sunlight and water and animals fight for food, water and shelter.

Cave men

From the emergence of human existence winning was a priority. The basis for winning any battle is shaped by merit.

If you didn't compete you were not as viable as others around you. Viability was based on the chances you took to survive. The basis for natural selection would become inevitably rooted in merit.

In general, the males as hunter gathers ventured out from the safety of the group and returned with something of value. Assuming they had the wherewithal to find their way back, their goal was to bring food, water or directions to a better place for their group to call home. Shelter next to, water, a lake or stream with plenty of naturally growing fruits and vegetables was an ultimate setting.

This type of environment was a prime place for animals to gather and forage thus making it a fine hunting ground.

Learning skills, such as making tools, throwing a spear, atlatl or using a sling to bring down prey was essential to survival. Knowing how to gut and clean your quarry so it wouldn't be contaminated was an inherent necessity. Teaching and learning in itself are forms of merit.

About the fourth or fifth time they returned to the group empty handed they would have initiated shunning. Shunned individuals would eventually completely fall out of favor with the group and would be sent off to fend for themselves.

Shunned individuals rarely procreated due to social dominance of alfa males in each group.

Alfa males usually had there pick of the women in the clan and a handful became favored. Those females, upon occasion, would defend the dominant male because they were a strong, worthy and proficient provider and protector.

The remaining male members in the clan would via for the next best in line and would often fight for the right to sire desirable females.

Periodically challenged by young and upcoming males a hierarchy would develop throughout the life span of the clan.

The best of the best females in the group were rarely sick, definitely were not weak and learned how to keep a dominate partner by catering to his needs.

Nesting was just as prevalent then as it is now. When the female was in heat nature would take its course.

Several months later she would start gathering twigs for a bed and placing them in a sheltered location. Under the canopy of several trees, under a ledge or in a cave.

Letting her obsess with these matters was a wise decision. If momma ain't happy ain't nobody happy.

Balancing rearing children, keeping the fire going and in general providing a more comfortable existence would tend to earn her a more comfortable position in the clan.

Preparing food, making clothing and keeping their dwelling protected and in order were skills they learned from their mothers or by watching other females in the tribe.

Before all you modern women get too bent out of shape about the pre-described arrangement. This is a generalization, and upon occasion these roles were reversed.

All in all, this rash broad-brush stroke depicts the commonplace roles that earned individuals their place in their community.

As a young child your world would have been fairly carefree. Clinging to mother's breast and later constantly underfoot, unless mom had to get something done. Then you had better look out and stay out of her way.

Assessing Where You Want to Be

Wants, Needs & Desires
What are they and why prioritization is important?

Miriam/Webster says
Want:
1: to fail to possess especially in customary or required amount : LACK the
answer *wanted* courtesy
2a: to have a strong desire for *wanted* a chance to rest
b: to have an inclination to : LIKE say what you *want*, he is efficient
3a: to have need of : REQUIRE the motor *wants* a tune-up
b: to suffer from the lack of thousands still *want* food and shelter
4: OUGHT —used with the infinitive you *want* to be very careful what you say— Claudia Cassidy
5: to wish or demand the presence of
6: to hunt or seek in order to apprehend *wanted* for murder

Need:
1: necessary duty : OBLIGATION no *need* to apologize the *need* to pay taxes— Peter Scott
2a: a lack of something requisite, desirable, or useful a building adequate for the company's *needs*
b: a physiological or psychological requirement for the well-being of an organism health and education *needs*
3: a condition requiring supply or relief. the house is in *need* of repair. refugees in *need* of shelter and food
4: lack of the means of subsistence : POVERTY The community program provides for those in *need*.

Desire:
1: conscious impulse (see IMPULSE_ENTRY_1_SENSE 1) toward something that promises enjoyment or satisfaction in its attainment ridding oneself of all *desire* show humans process *desire*
2a: LONGING, CRAVING teenagers' *desire* for independence… the

inexpensive homebuilt craft that satisfy many people's *desire* to fly— James Fallows
b: sexual urge or appetite
3: something longed or hoped
for : something <u>desired</u> You are my
heart's *desire.*
4: a usually formal request or petition for some action

What Are Your Values

There are three basic types of values. Character, Work and Personal
1.   **Character values** are the values one needs to possess in order to exist in society as a good upstanding citizen. Like; Respect, Commitment, Positive attitude and loyalty.
2.   **Work Values** are the attributes you want to have in order to exist professionally. Like; Stability, Prestige, Capabilities and Communication.
3.   **Personal Values** are what define you as a person. Like Personality, Health, Family, Appearance and Popularity.

Link: https://winningfutures.org/mentor/three-types-values-students-explore/

Everything Fun Has a Cost

No matter what fun thing you choose to do, there's nearly always a drawn back.

As for instance if you like rollercoasters so much you could ride them all day – if you could afford it.

Or you love to go fishing, decisions, decisions, where's the best lake, what bait is working today, how do I get there, do I need, a license, a boat, a truck to pull it, an outboard motor, a trolling motor and what are the costs?

You nearly always have to do something else first.

"I find that the harder I work, the more luck I seem to have."

-- Thomas Jefferson

Goals

Do goals have merit? Most say they probably do, however there are always the inevitable pessimists.

Why set goals if they only set you up for failure? Why walk around in a dream world when you know you'll not be rewarded for your efforts.

Goals many times are so huge they seem unattainable. Most people don't know where to start. I believe if you break them down into smaller achievable goals, rest assured, you'll start at the beginning.

Well, let's look into it a little deeper. Goal number 1, I want to be a millionaire. Understanding that just wishing or wanting it, is not going to achieve this lofty goal. One must break it down into smaller segments or smaller goals if you'll have it.

Ok, I want to be a hundredaire. Seems easier already, doesn't it. Some would say absurd however logic would dictate a hundredaire would have to come first. Then a thousandaire, tenthousandaire and so on. Like rungs on a ladder, to achieve new heights, a person must ascend gradually. Realizing it would be difficult, if not impossible, to start at the top rung of the ladder, setting your goals in smaller increments becomes infinitely clearer.

TPS (Toyota Production Systems)

What is TPS and how can I personally benefit from it in my life. TPS is "Toyota

Production Systems" and is a system developed back in the late 40's that have created todays "LEAN PRICIPALS" in manufacturing.

How is that going to help me, you ask. Again, just like Six Sigma (described later) the principals of self-improvement and lean manufacturing are very similar.

1. Define the Value
2. Map Value Stream
3. Create Flow
4. Establish Pull
5. Pursuit perfection

Utilizing a decade's old tried and true formula to achieve continuous improvement is a marvelous way to establish merit in your life.

In this case again we will transfer manufacturing processes to personal building blocks that will work for you in molding a better approach to achievements in your life.

1. Identify the value of your assignment, task and or goal.
2. Lay out a plan as to how you are going to achieve that value. Break it down into simple steps.
3. Start at the beginning and follow through to completion. If one of the simple tasks is too complex break it down into smaller tasks. Eliminate wasteful tasks.
4. Establish a personal pull system. The goal of the system is to best manage the amount of work you take on at any given time.
5. This stage presents the ability to revisit the first four stages and tweak their performance. Make improvements, consolidate steps and remove extra steps. Undoubtedly this is a system that you will repeat over and over again in your life and getting better at it is a stellar goal.

Building a personal task board, hanging it on the wall or having a virtual copy on your phone or in your computer will make certain you don't overbook your schedule.

This could be as simple as a daily or weekly chart or as complex as monthly or even yearly. Establish a timeline for each goal or task and only move them to a later date if you have to.

If for some reason something unexpected should occur that stops you from completing a task, pull one from the future to make best use of your time.

Remember these are flexible tools and are meant to be fluid or in a constant state of flux.

Six Sigma

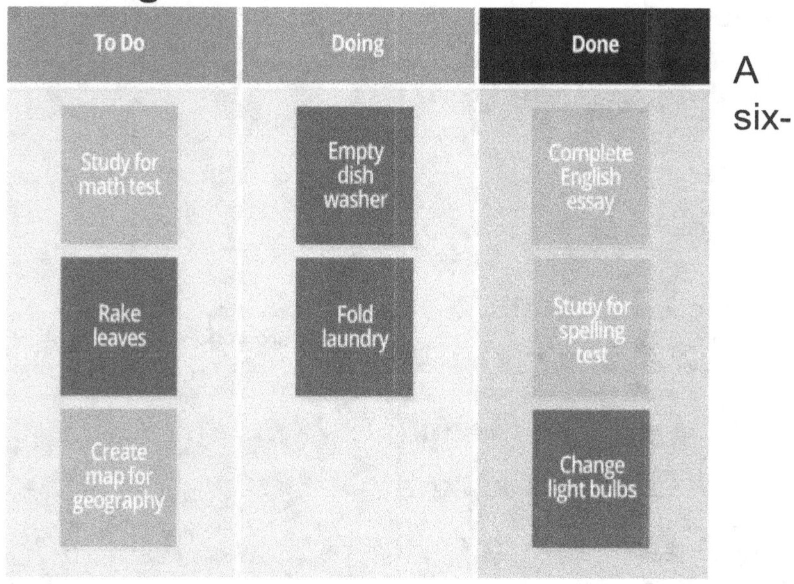

A six- sigma process is one in which 99.99966% of all opportunities to produce some feature of a part are statistically expected to be free of defects. (Not meant to be used to achieve perfection but, to get a step closer to it.)

The 7 key Six Sigma principles are:

A six-sigma process is one in which 99.99966% of all opportunities to produce some feature of a part are statistically expected to be free of defects. This relates to your plan or goal you wish to complete.

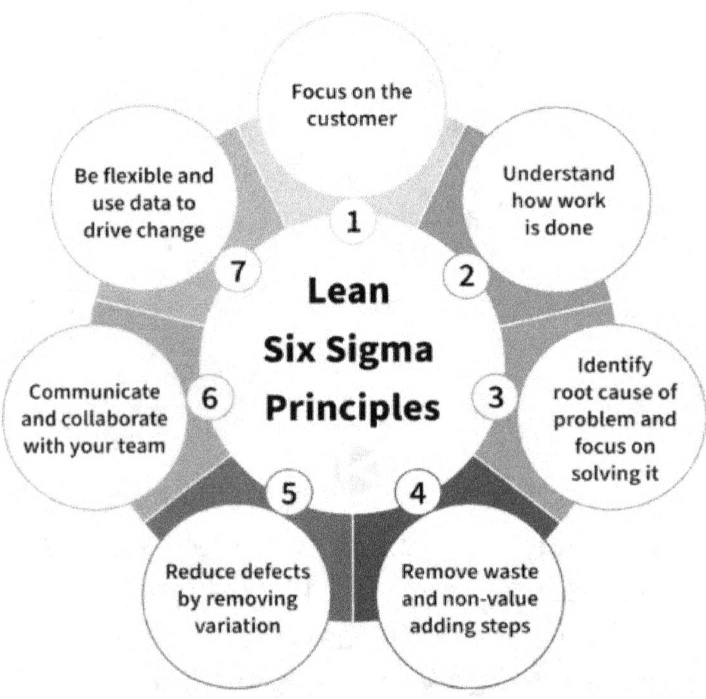

1. Always focus on the customer. **Even if the customer is you.**
2. Understand how work really happens. **Research how to obtain your goal**.
3. Make your processes flow smoothly. **Arrange your tasks in order.**

4. Reduce waste and concentrate on value. **Remove deterrents and distractions.**
5. Stop defects through removing variation. **Make your plan simple and stick to it.**
6. Get buy-in from the team through collaboration. **Talk it over with people that have achieved your goal or are involved in your decision.**
7. Make your efforts systematic and scientific. **Always map out your plan on paper, phone or computer.**

How to use Six-Sigma to enhance your personal wellbeing. Although constructed for manufacturing the principals are all the same. In this scenario "Them" would be an individual, individuals, group, groups and or entity.

1. Always focus on those you wish to influence.
2. Understand how they think and how to appeal to their sense of how you will make life better for them.
3. A smooth flow of information between you and them is key to bringing them in.
4. Remove all obstacles that stand in the way of meeting your goals.

5. Hone your communication skills to become as consistent as possible.
6. Convincing them that with you, life will get easier, happier, richer etc.

Be methodical and meticulous, use facts.

Based on Six Sigma Principles DMAIC Define, Measure, Analyze, Improve, Control.

- **Attainable; (Define)**

Make sure your goal is attainable. There is no better way to set yourself up for failure then to set you goals too high. Be practical. There's nothing wrong with having a wonderful dream however, make sure you know what path will be necessary in order to get from where you are today to where you want to be in the future.

Whatever your goal might be, whether it would be something as simple as to lose a certain amount of weight or to become a rocket scientist or brain surgeon.

Remember having more than one goal is a doable situation. As a matter of fact, it's a great idea but, make sure you know how to attain a goal before multi-tasking.

It might be a good idea to start with smaller easier to achieve goals and work your way up to harder ones and then multiple goals.

- **Prioritize; (Measure)**

Just like rungs on a ladder, map out the steps it will take to achieve your goal. There will almost always be several steps you need to research, compile and assemble in a proper order. As a for instance a goal of losing weight, diet and exercise would be essential elements in attaining your goal.

You need to realize that you're not going to be able to just snap your fingers and boom you're there. Knowing the number of calories, you need to gain, maintain and lose weight for a person of your size and gender.

Setting a number of pounds, you would like to lose. Collecting the proper data of what foods and quantities of those foods are required in order to reach your goal.

Say you'd like to lose fifty pounds make sure that would be a healthy weight for you and how long it should take to safely lose that amount.

Find what exercises burn how many calories and identify the parts of your body you would like to improve.

Now you can map out a schedule detailing your meals and exercises and coordinate it with a reasonable timeline.

Once you've got all your information you can implement your plan.

- **Act; (Analyze)**

Now that you have a plan the time has come to take action. Don't be afraid, if you don't know where to start. Rest assured no matter where you start it will be at the beginning.

It's not a bad idea to keep a daily log to document your actions. It can be as simple as a daily check list or as complex as writing down everything you are doing to get from where you are today to where you'd like to be in the future.

As an example; did you exercise? Yes or No or go into detail as to what exercises you have done, how many repetitions and what you had for every meal and snack throughout your day. Detailing calories burned and consumed including weight scale readings.

- **Upgrade; (Improve)**
Using the information, you compile you can then document your progress.

Remember if you backslide or fall off track of attaining your goal doesn't make you a failure.

Dust yourself off and get back with the program as soon as possible.

Your plan isn't carved in stone. You may not reach the goals set forth in your plan within the restraints of your timeline or you may be ahead of schedule.

If this is the case, take a step back, analyze, assess, evaluate, adjust and move forward.

There is nothing wrong with not following your plan to the nth degree as long as you're improving.

Remember if you're moving toward your goal, you are accomplishing something you hadn't done before and you should feel good about doing so.

- **Maintain; (Control)**

Once you become accustom to the cadence of your plan, stick to it and continue to get better at executing the individual segments of your schedule.

It's important that maintain forward motion (progress) in order to reach the desired state, you've set out to achieve.

- **Repeat; (Reappraise)**
Every time you go through this regiment, you should be able to see improvement. If you don't, go back and start over and make certain you have made improvements.

"Energy and persistence conquer all things."
- Benjamin Franklin.

"Good Enough, is Not Finished"

Emulate

I've got five words for you. Learn, learn, learn, learn and learn!

The day I stop learning will be the day I start pushing up daisies.

Make yourself a sponge for new things. Let absorbing knowledge with every turn in your life a way of life. Whatever it is that interests you, look it up find out more about it, study it and know it.

There is nothing more gratifying than learning something new and accomplishing something with that knowledge.

For example, if you want to become an astronaut, look up several astronauts and find out the steps they took in order to become an astronaut then follow in their footsteps.

People don't just sign up for these goals and instantly they are there.

Most folks that achieve greatness in their specific field generally don't get there by happenstance. They plan and work hard and plan some more and little at a time they eventually get there.

No matter if you want to be a rocket scientist, brain surgeon, astronaut or just a good parent. You shouldn't want to settle for being good. You should strive to be great at whatever it is you'd like to become.

The least that can come out of that type of goal, is that you will be the best you can be at whatever it is that you set your sights on.

Weeds in your garden

Maybe the time has come to measure where you are and where you'd like to be.

What things could possibly stand in the way of growing your potential?

1.   Vision; The first thing you need to do is to set a goal. It's quite easy, just take a piece of paper and write it down. Then step by step create a plan of how you're going to get there.

2.   Focus; One of the most frequent deterrents are distractions. I like to set aside a time, let's just say an hour, in your busy day to be alone. While you have this time, make use of it to clear your head and flesh out your plan.

3.   Willpower; Use revisiting the vision and focus on parts of your goal to rekindle that fire and forge onward to the next step toward your goal.

4.   Attempting to make everyone happy. Remember while enacting your plan you can satisfy most people some of the time and some people most the time, but never all the people all of the time. It's important to analyze if there is a finite audience or whether a broad-brush stroke of individuals will best fit your end goal.

5.   Being Frightened; Fear should never be underestimated. It's one of the most common

factors in not meeting one's goals. Fear of failure.

 "A person who never made a
mistake never tried anything new."
– Albert Einstein

6.   Fear of rejection. One of the most ominous fears of all. We all make mistakes; they are more common than you think. If they cost you, in time, money or ego, I chalk them up as a valuable lesson and move on. Remember nothing of any value is normally obtained without an element of risk.
7.   Average Mentality; Although there's absolutely nothing wrong with being average, settling for average frequently hinders success. Our desire to go beyond where we have been in the past is what keeps us pushing our boundary's. Continuous improvement should become your partner in your stride toward the next level.
8.   Attempt at Perfection; This is a hurdle that causes many to get stuck in an eternal vortex of starting parts of your plan over and over again. Striving for perfection is not a bad thing however, there is no such thing as

perfect. If you wait for your plan to be perfect before you enact it, you may be waiting for a very long time. I like to measure it by examining whether or not I've got it arranged better than I've ever had it before.

"If you want something you've never had, you must be willing to do something you've never done."
-       *Thomas Jefferson*

Personal Space

How important is personal space to those around you?

Personal space is something that we all have. However, there are multiple factors that influence the differing distances of one's personal space. These factors include gender, age, and culture, among others (Tolley). Males interacting with other males require the most personal space (Gifford, 1987).

Personal space is to be considered as the distance between people in a social, family or work environment. Imagine it to be an invisible shield that surrounds everyone's physical being.

If you question how deeply rooted in our internal makeup the value of personal space is, try this. Sit in your father's space at the dinner table, sit at the geek's or in-folk's table in the lunchroom or crawl into your partners side of the bed, then just wait for the reaction. Sparks will fly or it will, at least, strike up a lively discussion.

Personal space begins at around arm's length during an average social conversation.

I find it intrusive when people stand too close to me or speak to me with their face about ten inches from mine. Many people don't like to be touched, other than quite possibly a hearty handshake.

Some people are touchy feely kind of people. It's ok, there are many different personality types but, what do you do if someone occupies your personal space.

a. Ask them if they could give you a little room.
b. Be cautious how you phrase your request.
c. Be mindful it may be your personality type.

   d. Remind them of why you're so close. (I asked you over here to talk about our plan)

   e. Make it a point to reconvene your conversation.

Personal Potential

In other words, self-growth, self-improvement or personal growth as a way to achieve your goals by improving your knowledge, communication skills and personal qualities.

These may be a means to attain an enhanced environment through increasing employment opportunities and financial gain ultimately leading to better surroundings i. e. living location, house, food, clothing, vehicle and the like.

   a. Start today.

   b. Get up early.

   c. Strengthen self-confidence.

   d. Seek those with knowledge of what you need to learn and listen to them.

e. Welcome change. Forge through fears until you're comfortable without them. Make them your friend.

f. Practice presentations. Work on visual expressions as well as spoken.

g. Move away from the negative things in your life.

h. Challenge yourself. Shed old habits and replace them with newer better ones.

i. Be Passionate about achieving your goals.

j. Make good decisions.

k. Never stop improving. Never give up.

Responsibility

To admit it was your fault, is to take responsibility. To blame ones-self for making a poor choice or choices. To become accountable, amenable, answerable, and liable.

When is it time to take responsibility?

How do I take responsibility?

a. Don't blame others.

b. Don't make excuses.

c. How does what you've done affect others.

d. Don't beat yourself up over it.

e. Stop being negative.
f. Accepting negative happenings as part of life.
g. Be Positive and finish what you start.
     Pause, analyze, repeat a thru g, sustain.

Taking it personally

Failure, Rejection, Criticism and Perseverance Why you shouldn't take it personal.
     When something hits a nerve and you begin to think others see your doubts and insecurities. You think they dislike you for the very same reasons you dislike yourself. You assume they can't comprehend you're capable of carrying through with the things that intimidate you.
     a. Question your beliefs
     b. Don't worry what others think.
     c. Don't think it's all about you.
     d. Build self-confidence.
     e. Don't give negative thoughts free rent in your head.
     f. Find something else to do, rather than stew.
     g. Stay calm, change the subject in your head.

h. Don't take anything personally. There are twice as many opinions in the world as there are idiots.
i. Be happy with who you are regardless.

Fortitude

The mental strength and courage that allows someone to face danger, pain etc.
   a. courage. The quality of a confident character.
   b. determination (related) A decision arrived at by thought and investigation; conclusion.
   c. mettle. The ability to meet a challenge or persevere under demanding circumstances; determination or resolve:
   d. perseverance.
   e. braveness.
   f. stoicism.
   g. strength.
   h. endurance.

Integrity

1: firm adherence to a code of especially moral or artistic values: incorruptibility. 2: an unimpaired condition: soundness. 3: the quality or state of being complete or undivided: completeness.

> a. Honesty. This means telling the truth, being open, not taking advantage of others. ...
> b. Respect. ...
> c. Generating trust. ...
> d. Pride. ...
> e. Responsibility. ...
> f. Keeping promises. ...
> g. Helping others.

Create a Goal Pyramid

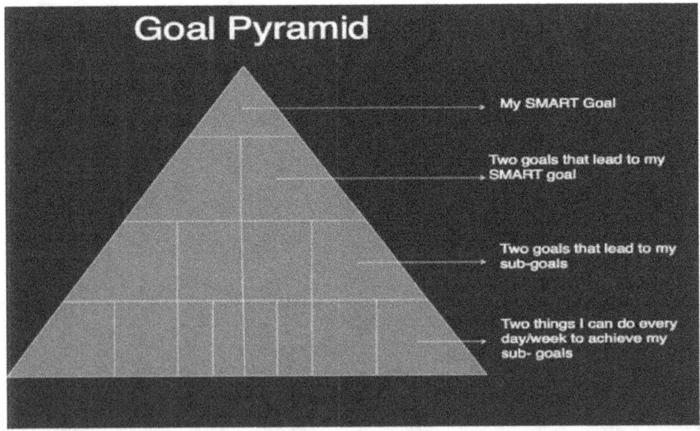

Have a workable plan. Study how others in a similar situation to yours attained a similar goal. Emulating the success of others is great place to start. Understanding that thousands of people have reached the goal you are seeking, gives you plenty of study material.

One thing I learned, as I grew, is that it's frequently a numbers game.

A friend of mine wanted to start a concrete hauling business. I thought it to be odd in that there were already eight other companies doing the same thing in his area. I believed there would be too steep of competition to succeed.

My friend pointed out, if there were only two others doing it in his vicinity competition may be greater. I asked him, "How's that?" He answered, "if there was only two, maybe there wasn't room for a third were as with eight others a ninth would more than likely fit in easier.

It gave my great pause but, I had to agree with him. All he would have to do is deliver a little faster or a tiny bit less expensive and there would be a niche, then he would be able slip in fairly unnoticed by his competitors.

There are only 3 things for sale. Concepts, Ideas and Dreams

Concepts; Concepts are defined as abstract ideas or general notions that occur in the mind, in speech, or in thought. ... In contemporary philosophy, there are prevailing ways to understand what
a concept is: Concepts as mental representations, where concepts are entities that exist in the mind (mental objects)

Ideas; Merriam Webster
\ ī-ˈdē-ə, -ˈdēə *also* ˈī-(ˌ)dē-ə *or* ˈī-dē \
Definition of *idea*
1: a formulated thought or opinion
2: whatever is known or supposed about something
3: the central meaning or chief end of a particular action or situation
4a: a plan for action: DESIGN
b: a standard of perfection: IDEAL
c: a transcendent entity that is a real pattern of which existing things are imperfect representations

Dreams;
Definition of *dream*
 (Entry 1 of 2)

1: a series of thoughts, images, or emotions occurring during sleep had a *dream* about climbing a mountain gives me bad *dreams*— compare REM SLEEP
2: an experience of <u>waking</u> life having the characteristics of a dream: such as
a: a visionary
(see VISIONARY_ENTRY_1_SENSE 2A)
creation of the imagination : DAY DREAM the *dreams* of her youth
b: a state of mind marked by abstraction or release from reality : REVERIE walking around in a *dream*
c: an object seen in a dreamlike state : VISION a man that was her *dream* come true
3: something notable for its beauty, excellence, or enjoyable quality the new car is a *dream* to operate
4a: a strongly desired goal or purpose a *dream* of becoming president
b: something that fully satisfies a wish : IDEAL a meal that was a gourmet's *dream*

How to get there from here when you're actually nowhere at all.

Reality is to dream and dreams are what reality is made from. The ones who just sit there and expect great things to happen are, more often than not, the ones that end up just sitting there.

All great wants and desires are brought to fruition, born of dreams, concepts and ideas. Dreams, concepts and ideas are the only things in the world that are for sale. No matter what it is that one wants in life it starts with these and usually grows into a plan of what obstacles or sacrifices one will have to make in order to obtain what they envision.

Examples:

1.   Drawing a picture, in their mind or on paper of what you will make for them.
2.   Getting them to picture themselves in a new suit, car or house.
3.   The idea of them being a slimmer more attractive individual.
4.   Presenting them with details that will benefit them, their family or company.

Words have merit.

Most people in the world are visual. They imagine things with pictures in their minds.

If you tell your children, "Don't leave your plate on the table when you're done eating." The word pictures that stick in their minds, "leave plate" and "on table". Instead learn to rephrase your sentence like; When you're done eating put your dishes in the sink or dish washer. Then they picture dishes in the sink or in the dish washer.

Keep in mind there are very few mind pictures that depict negative words like "no, nothing, won't, don't or not."

The absence of part of, or all of something or the presence of nothing is extremely difficult for most to picture. When someone says; Mom's not at home, you most likely picture your mom and your home and not that she's not there.

Emotions on the other hand come from deeper within. Stirring one's emotions are usually more complex than telling or asking someone to be happy, sad, laugh or cry and ever far more of a convoluted enigma to get them to love or hate.

Although you can paint pictures in their minds in the form of a story to bring out such emotions, the picture that becomes present in individuals minds when you say "Love" or "Hate" is commonly as different as the people themselves.

As for instance; the Japanese have no word for love. It's even difficult to describe love in English without going into a long explanation.

Words like sorrow may bring to mind, for an individual, a time when that emotion filled their very being. Such as the death of a loved one, a close friend or a pet. Sorrow could be as simple as moving out of a house you lived in or selling a car that you owned for many years.

Compassion and empathy are deeply engrained emotions that are typically environmental as well as learned.

These feelings take on as many shapes in one's mind as there are grains of sand on the beach.

The best communicators are ones that can paint word picture stories in others minds.

Is there a formula for getting what you want in the world? Of course, there is. How does a child get the attention of their mother or father? In the beginning not being able to express themselves in words, they cry. So too hot, too cold, hunger and discomfort all get vocalized loudly and mom or dad respond.

In that parents find this frustrating or annoying they set forth to modify that behavior. They are on their way, followed by a series of grunts, groans, giggles and coos and next facial expressions and hand gestures. Reaching out for wanting and pushing away for not wanting.

With smiles and frowns they banter back and forth and gradually form methods understandable and palatable to everyone involved. These are conditioned responses that children get pretty good at. Although they find quickly, they don't always get what they want, they ordinarily get plenty of what they didn't even realize they wanted.

Food in their tummy's, clothes on their backs, a roof over their heads and an abundance of loving care and affection.

Soon they develop the skills of the best sales staff known to mankind. Tugging at your heart strings with every whim and desire. Not wanting to disappoint, parents are saddled with a complicated decision-making process. Seems a fourth-floor apartment at the corner of 44th and Wadsworth is not the proper environment for a pony and a goldfish isn't a good compromise. Anyway, gerbils or guinea pigs do the trick, well, at least until they find the rat poison.

Communication;

Selling in the real world. Sell yourself first.
     Selling many times has negative connotations.
1.   The high-pressure car salesman.
2.   The door to door salesman placing their foot in the door.
3.   Those pesky pop-up ads that interfere with dang near anything you attempt to do online.
4.   Those robo-calls about your car warrantee expiring.

     Ugh, what a nightmare. Who in the heck wants to be affiliated with that bunch of obnoxious rhetoric? "Not me". Said just about everyone.

Well I'm here to tell you, it's not like that. The real world dictates we become good communicators to get by. Whether your applying for a job, wanting to go on a date or simply needing the salt from across the table, selling oneself is going to be paramount in winning them over.

One thing that really sticks in my craw is when people demand things. Being demanding, even if you are the boss, is taken as a threat by many. Pass you the salt, or you'll what, I ponder. Imagine you wish to go on a date with that fascinating individual you just met and you tell them you're going to take them to a movie or diner. Do you think you'd get the date? Probably not.

There is a simple method I use that smooths everything out. I ask.

Will you please pass me the salt?

May I take you out on a date?

Would you like to see a movie?

Would you like to meet me for diner?

No matter how amazingly talented or skilled you are, you will have a difficult time getting where you want to go if you don't know how to sell yourself to others.

- How do you communicate your value to others?
- Talented folks still have to sell themselves to succeed.
- You aren't going to suddenly get discovered if you don't make an effort to sell yourself.
- You should show others who you really are. Don't be afraid.
- An ethical and honest approach is the easiest way.
- It's within your rights to occupy a portion of this world just like everyone else.
- Promoting yourself is to emphasize your strengths, not to take unfair advantage of others weaknesses.
- Highlight how your talents and skills will benefit others in any situation.
- Everyone depends on selling themselves to a certain degree, even in everyday life.

Communicating is more than just words.

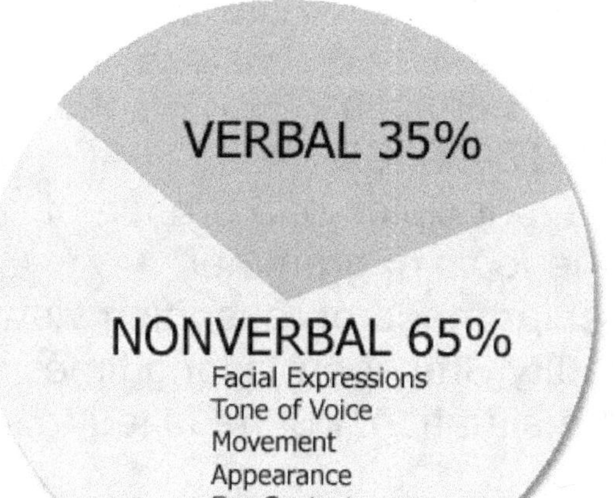

Know who you're selling to. Four Basic

Personalities

Analytical, Expressive, Driver, Amiable

Definitions that may help you identify the different personality types.

Logic (Analytical)

Definition of *logic Merriam Webster*
1a(1): a science that deals with the principles and criteria of validity of <u>inference</u> and demonstration : the science of the formal principles of reasoning a professor of *logic*

(2): a branch or variety of logic modal *logic* Boolean *logic*

(3): a branch of semiotics
specially : SYNTACTICS

(4): the formal principles of a branch of knowledge the *logic* of grammar

b(1): a particular mode of reasoning viewed as valid or faulty She spent a long time explaining the situation, but he failed to see her *logic*.

(2): RELEVANCE, PROPRIETY could not understand the *logic* of such an action

c: interrelation or sequence of facts or events when seen as inevitable or predictable By the *logic* of events, anarchy leads to dictatorship.

d: the arrangement of circuit elements (as in a computer) needed for computation
also : the circuits themselves

2: something that forces a decision apart from or in opposition to reason the *logic* of war

Emotion (Expressive)

Definition of *emotion Merriam Webster*
1a: a conscious mental reaction (such as anger or fear) subjectively experienced as strong feeling usually directed toward a

specific object and typically accompanied by physiological and behavioral changes in the body
b: a state of feeling
c: the affective aspect of consciousness : FEELING

2a: EXCITEMENT

Tactic (Driver)
Definition of *tactic Meriam Webster*
 (Entry 1 of 3)
1: a device for accomplishing an end
2: a method of employing forces in combat
tactic
 adjective
Definition of *tactic* (Entry 2 of 3)
: of or relating to arrangement or order
-tactic
 adjective combining form
Definition of *-tactic* (Entry 3 of 3)
1: of, relating to, or having (such) an arrangement or pattern phono*tactic*
2: showing orientation or movement directed by a (specified) force or agent geo*tactic*

Amiable

Definition of *amiable Meriam Webster*
1a: friendly, sociable, and <u>congenial</u>
an *amiable* host *amiable* neighbors
b: generally agreeable an *amiable* comedy

2*archaic* : PLEASING, ADMIRABLE

Know the people you're trying to influence.
I look at the four types, not as quadrants but as a

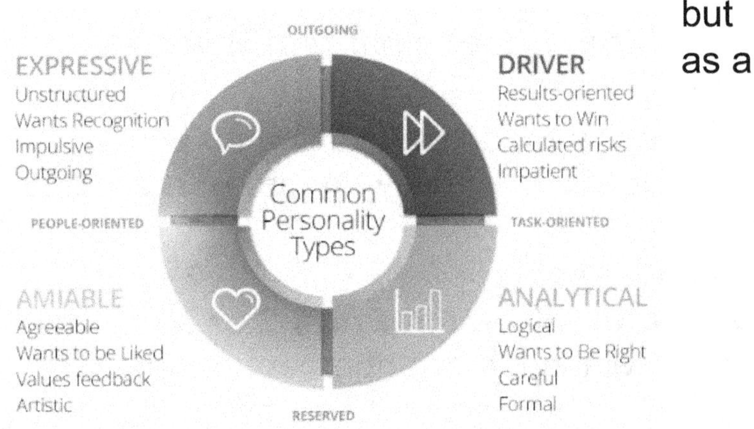

blend moving from one to the next as we go around the circle.

I like to look at this matrix as a circle because in my mind it creates a bell curve. The lighter central portion creating 50% of the total and then diminishes as we move toward the outer fringe.

2D Bell Curve Fig. 1

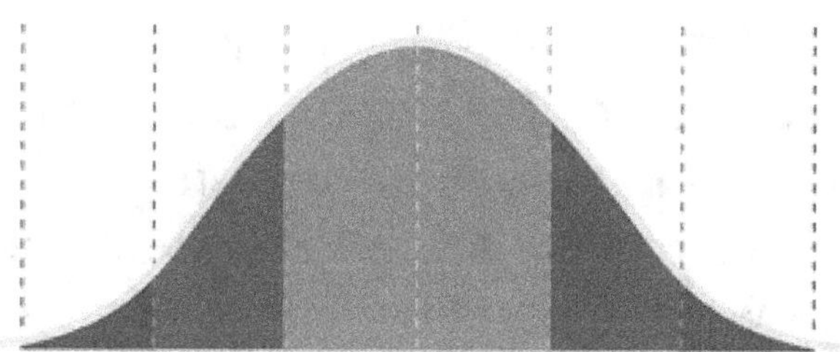

     Now if we take that blend and sweep it around to make a 3D Bell Curve. More truly like a bell. We can now see how everyone's personality type might fall in a unique spot on that bell representing our entire population.
3D Bell Curve Fig. 2

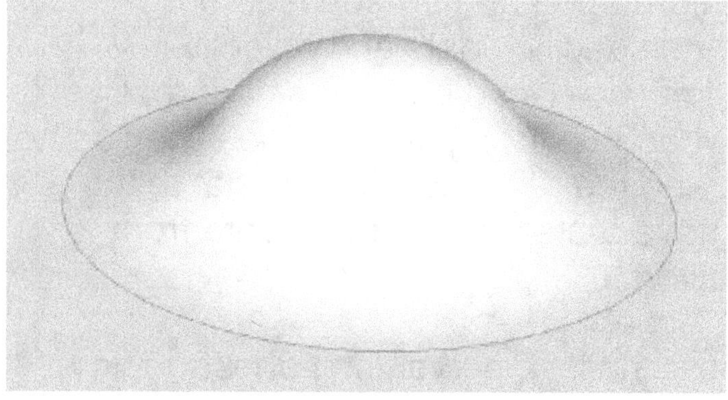

     The majority of people fall in the somewhere in the center of the bell and as personalities become more extreme, they move toward the less populated fringe. The perfectly well balanced would occupy the very center of the bell. Most are comprised of some of each of the types and yet it is nearly impossible to be 100% of any one type.

Learning to read these personality types gives you a distinct advantage when it come to the powers of persuasion. Remember convincing others to accept you for who and what you are worth is the key to succeeding through merit.

According to Rhys Metler

1. The Driver:
This personality type is assertive. They want a lot of information and are focused on achieving specific goals and objectives. Sometimes they can present as aggressive, even when they don't mean to be. They do not like having their time wasted, so get to the point, have a plan, and differentiate from competitors.

2. The Amiable:
This personality type values honesty. They are looking to develop an ongoing business relationship, so establishing trust and rapport is essential. Expect them to take more time to make decisions. They prefer a step by step process rather than you providing everything

up front. Communicate how your product has helped others and provide testimonials.

3. The Analytical:

This personality type focuses on the numbers. They will be prepared and will research you just as much as you have researched them before your meeting. They make decisions based on facts, so playing to their emotions will not work. Provide the key benefits, and back up all your claims with facts and stats.

4. The Expressive:

This personality type can be impulsive and doesn't like getting bogged down in the details. They tend to be open and energetic. They are open to establishing long term partnerships. Sell them by offering case studies that demonstrate your product's track record of success.

<u>Excerpt from</u> https://www.salesforcesearch.com
Naturally, not all people will fit perfectly into these categories, so be cognizant of their dominant personality type(s) and skew your sales tactics to connect with them on that level. While it may take some time to feel people out and get a grasp of their personality, it will be well worth it when you establish a connection and close the deal.

Sixteen Personality Types
Myers & Briggs have taken it to another level.   If you wish, it is recommended you look deeper into personality types. The more you know the better off you will be. Myers & Briggs use these eight identifiers in combination to build their sixteen types.

Extroverts
are energized by people, enjoy a variety of tasks, a quick pace, and are good at multitasking.

Introverts
often like working alone or in small groups, prefer a more deliberate pace, and like to focus on one task at a time.

Sensors
are realistic people who like to focus on the facts and details, and apply common sense and past experience to come up with practical solutions to problems.

Intuitives
prefer to focus on possibilities and the big picture, easily see patterns, value innovation, and seek creative solutions to problems.

Thinkers
tend to make decisions using logical analysis, objectively weigh pros and cons, and value honesty, consistency, and fairness.

Feelers
tend to be sensitive and cooperative, and decide based on their own personal values and how others will be affected by their actions.

Judgers
tend to be organized and prepared, like to make and stick to plans, and are comfortable following most rules.

Perceivers
prefer to keep their options open, like to be able to act spontaneously, and like to be flexible with making plans.

In various combinations they create 16 Types

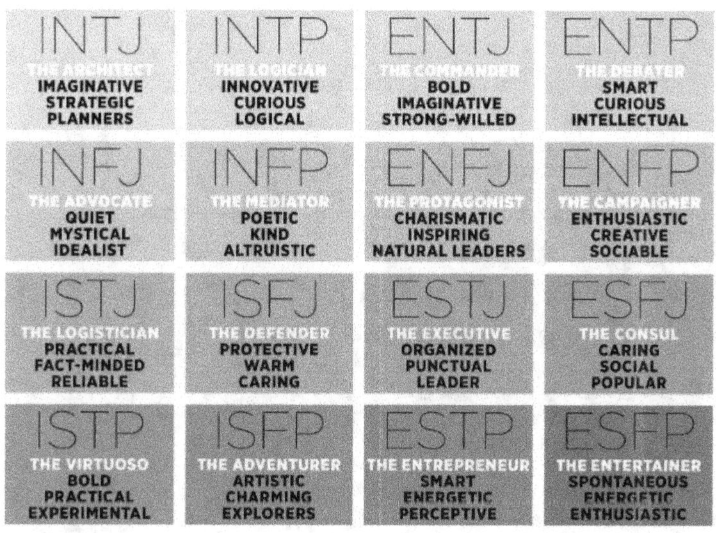

ENTJ The Commander Strategic leaders, motivated to organize change

INTJ The Mastermind Analytical problem-solvers, eager to improve systems and processes

ENTP The Visionary Inspired innovators, seeking new solutions to challenging problems

INTP The Architect Philosophical innovators, fascinated by logical analysis

ENFJ The Teacher Idealist organizers, driven to do what is best for humanity

INFJ The Counselor Creative nurturers, driven by a strong sense of personal integrity

ENFP The Champion People-centered creators, motivated by possibilities and potential

INFP The Healer Imaginative idealists, guided by their own values and beliefs

ESTJ The Supervisor Hardworking traditionalists, taking charge to get things done

ISTJ The Inspector Responsible organizers, driven to create order out of chaos

ESFJ The Provider Conscientious helpers, dedicated to their duties to others

ISFJ The Protector Industrious caretakers, loyal to traditions and institutions

ESTP The Dynamo Energetic thrill seekers, ready to push boundaries and dive into action

ISTP The Craftsperson Observant troubleshooters, solving practical problems

ESFP The Entertainer Vivacious entertainers, loving life and charming those around them

ISFP The Composer Gentle caretakers, enjoying the moment with low-key enthusiasm

Personality Type Distribution in the General Population

Type	Frequency in Population	
ISFJ	■■■■■■■■■■■■■■	13.8%
ESFJ	■■■■■■■■■■■■	12.3%
ISTJ	■■■■■■■■■■■■	11.6%
ISFP	■■■■■■■■■	8.8%
ESTJ	■■■■■■■■■	8.7%
ESFP	■■■■■■■■■	8.5%
ENFP	■■■■■■■■	8.1%
ISTP	■■■■■	5.4%
INFP	■■■■	4.4%
ESTP	■■■■	4.3%
INTP	■■■	3.3%
ENTP	■■■	3.2%
ENFJ	■■■	2.5%
INTJ	■■	2.1%
ENTJ	■■	1.8%
INFJ	■■	1.5%

Data source: "*MBTI Manual*" published by CPP

You more than likely are going to be selling to one of the top seven in the above chart. They represent 71.8 percent of the population.

These are the combinations that comprise every personality type their test reveals.

With practice you can learn to read people's faces. This is a technique utilized by law enforcement to catch people in a lie or to know when they are deceiving them.

Reading People's Faces

Now that you have a larger understanding about personalities you should next look at the ability to read people's faces.

Reading their face will provide you with insight as to their approval.

There are seven basic micro expressions you should learn. These expressions generally occur in a split second so you need to pay attention.

Tim Roth from "Lie to Me" TV Series demonstrates with detail.

1. Anger
2. Contempt
3. Disgust
4. Fear
5. Happiness
6. Sadness
7. Surprise

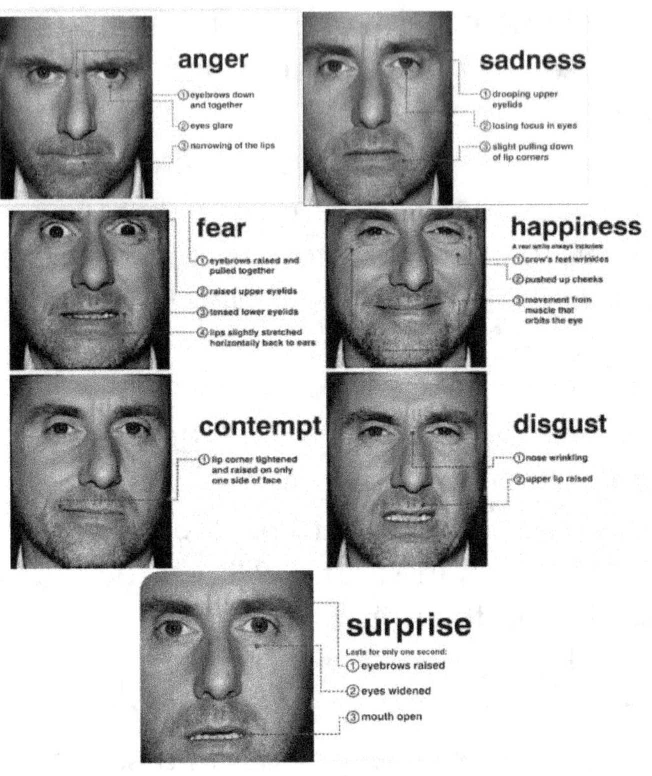

"Success is not the key to happiness. Happiness is the key to success. If you love what you are doing, you will be successful."
-- Albert Schweitzer

Find A Job You Love

They say, if you find a job you love, you'll never work a day in your life.

Anyone who's been in a relationship finds very quickly it's not all about you. There is a bit of give and take in order to harness the good you receive by participating in amiable joint venture.

Venturing headlong into the "pain and pleasure principal" of a long-term relationship can be a delicate balancing act. The one's where both sides give up less than they receive in return tend to be satisfyingly successful.

Typically, that is what is called a win-win situation. Whether that occurs in a personal relationship or a relationship between you and your job it should be the desired outcome.

Although that may be true, most people never find such an elusive artifact. That being, oft times the case what should a person do?

Consider things you're interested in and look for jobs in or around that interest.

For instance, if you like cars, let your mind wander. Are you artistic? Then design or detailing. This will unfold a myriad of jobs you may be suited for. Working in an automobile dealership or where they, ship or manufacture cars. Are you mechanical, fixing or repairing, maybe a body shop or engine rebuilding? Explore every aspect where a job intersects with cars.

If you like horses, do the same, veterinarian, grooming, a tac shop, working on a horse ranch. Believe me it will be nearly impossible to find a job you love 100% of however, take baby steps, get your foot in the door, so to speak. The more you learn, the more flexibility you'll earn, giving you a greater advantage to achieve that desirable position.

Look into career paths in that field and analyze where can it take you.

It's not always about the money but, you are the one that has to be comfortable with where the job will take you down the road.

Although I never understood not wanting to know more about one's endeavor, many are completely content with landing somewhere in the middle. We can't all be CEOs.

Make certain companies that exist in your field of choice generate company cultures you agree with.

Vegans probably won't fit in a beef packing plant and Sierra Club members may not want to pursue employment in coal or oil industries.

Make sure it makes sense in your life. Consider your desires and whether, or not, they coincide with your long-term goals.

Is the job a permanent stopping place or a stepping stone? One that teaches you essential skill in order to reach the next level in your career.

Find your purpose.

Sometimes it's difficult to find your passion. Surround yourself with people involved and interested in your field of intended expertise. Listen to those around you. Explore your interests. Look for down-sides and pitfalls in that arena. Examine whether they are something you can live with or change for the better.

Finally, give it a try first. You can always try something else. Do as much research as you can. Keep practicing. In order to obtain professional level skills, you'll need to have plenty of experience under your belt. Never quit. There isn't anyone that doesn't make any mistakes along the way.

My Jobs

My first job was laying sod for fifty cents an hour. I've had dozens of jobs. I pumped gas, was a short order cook, laborer, worked in a rendering plant, beef packing plant, assembly line worker, carpenter, roofer, bricklayer, drafter, salesman, engineer and CEO.

Most of these jobs came with a ton of baggage and not many had many silver linings. Yet all of them had something I was perfectly fine with, a paycheck.

And although absolutely every job had something I abhorred, they all taught me something I hadn't known before.

Most were very valuable lessons. In other words, they cost me. Delays, demotions, shame, embarrassment, being passed over for a promotion and yes even dismissal. YEP, I even got "Fired."

Vertical sale; Whether it be a **person, place or thing** trying to promote the idea of a vertical sale should come to mind. What is a vertical sale you ask?

For a **thing** it would be represented by an item in a similar market such as; if I was selling nails it would make sense for me to sell hammers as well because you may need one to use the other.

For a **place**; if I was in real estate and I bought furniture to stage a house for sale, it would be logical for me to sell the furniture to go with it as well.

For a **person;** if you're promoting yourself, no matter what market you are targeting, it is not for the shy, introverted or humble by any means. Branding is important. Be who you want to be. If to be known for a specific talent, make certain you are all you can be.

If a carpenter, reading blueprints, math and knowledge of lumber should be exhibited.

If a politician, civics, law and public speaking.

If a programmer, knowing different computer languages, software's and computers will definitely place you above others in your field.

Dusting off your past

Max Clausius - **"Present knowledge is wholly dependent on past knowledge"**

On the surface it is seemingly too simple to be true yet, every new avenue explored inevitably will find links to the past.

Example; It wasn't just one day someone decided to make a car. There was the wheel, then a wheelbarrow, then a two wheeled cart, then a wagon and that's just one avenue.
Next in 1680 Dutch physicist Christian Huygens experimented with an internal combustion engine, however no effective gasoline engine was developed until 1859.
Then in 1872, American George Brayton invented the first commercial liquid-fueled internal combustion engine.

There are hundreds of disciplines that contributed to eventually producing an automobile.

In that same respect we pick up tidbits of knowledge along the way that make us who we are today.

Given a specific goal, look into your own past to find those pieces of knowledge you can build on in order to propel you into the next level of understanding.

We learn as we go

Each day presents an opportunity to grow. We all grow in many ways. Emotionally, intellectually and in skills. Every hour of every day is filled with moments for you to excel. Be a sponge for knowledge.

There are basic streams of emotional intelligence. Self-awareness, Self-regulation, Motivation, Empathy and Social skills.

All of these combined in a proper balance are features that create how we fit in to society in general.

Take your field of interest. Have you learned anything about it today? Why? Is there any facet of it you don't thoroughly comprehend? Look it up. The internet and the library are limitless wells of information, go find out. Know the answers.

When was the last time you learned how to do something new? Or learned to do something better that you already knew how to do. It's never too late and you're never too old to learn. The day I stop learning will be the day I start pushing up daisies.

Some people go by the rules

In the early 70's I worked at a small machine shop in the mid-west. While working there, under the guidance of a brilliant engineer, we developed a process for manufacturing components for the snowmobile industry. The engineers at the company we were working for had their doubts about our succeeding with the methodology we were using. They hired an expert in the field of metal forming to go over our calculations to insure we would be able to meet their requirements. Compliance was a part contract in order to be paid. I must admit we were nervous because the machine had been already built.

After a lot of head scratching, pencil pushing and lengthy discussions. The, then $200/hr., engineer informed us, what we were attempting to do wasn't possible.

The chief engineer, plant owner and myself walked with the engineer to a shed out in back of the factory. I watched as the owner as he took the padlock off the hasp and slid the door open. The chief engineer looked at the compliance engineer and asked him. "So, how did we make all these parts then"?

The compliance engineer stood there wide eyed with his mouth hanging open. He then took the owner aside. As they talked, I couldn't hear what they were saying.

We locked up the shed and went back in the building. They called a meeting with all of the employees. The stoic compliance engineer took to the podium and began to speak. He went into great detail about his credentials and why the parent company had hired him to qualify our calculations and basically bless the machine we were about to deliver.

He concluded by identifying that the machine, by the numbers, did not meet the criteria. However, he went on to explain, some people go by the rules and some people make the rules.

It made me proud to be a member of the engineering team as he gave the machine a glowing report and signed off on its certification.

Rights https://www.un.org/en/global-issues/human-rights

There are 5 Basic Human Rights; the right to life and liberty, freedom from slavery and torture, freedom of opinion and expression, the right to work and education, and everyone is entitled to these rights, without discrimination.

There is a wealth of information online for a more in-depth view of these rights.

Understanding the meaning, risks and rewards of these are not key elements of survival is imperative in order establish merit in your current surroundings.

Risk and Reward

There are three basic types of risk and reward, Financial, Work and Personal

1. Financial; Depicts your short medium- and long-term monetary investments and analyzing the outcome based on estimates of what the future may bring.
2. Work; Planning strategies based on elements like. Should I change professions? Should I change jobs? Should I ask for that raise?

3. Personal; Is it time to go on a diet? Do I need more exercise? Should I ask that interesting person for a date?

Risk and Reward are linked, as a rule, with the concept of the greater the risk the greater the reward. However, there comes a point as to where the risk outweighs the reward.

HHHMMM How do you know where that point is?

Balancing risks and rewards are a learned art.

1.   Define what the reward is.
2.   Analyze the effect of the reward over the life span of the decision and determine how to measure the reward.

3.   Figure out how to examine the entire reward at the decision-making point of the process.
 Mapping out risk and reward.

Survival

Survival Needs: The truth is, there are only **five** basic **needs**; Clean Air, Water, Nutrients, Shelter and Sleep.
Delving deeper into the realm of survival essentials we look at Abraham Maslow's Pyramid.
Maslow's hierarchy of needs is an idea in psychology proposed by Abraham Maslow in his 1943 paper "A theory of Human

Motivation" in the journal Psychological Review.

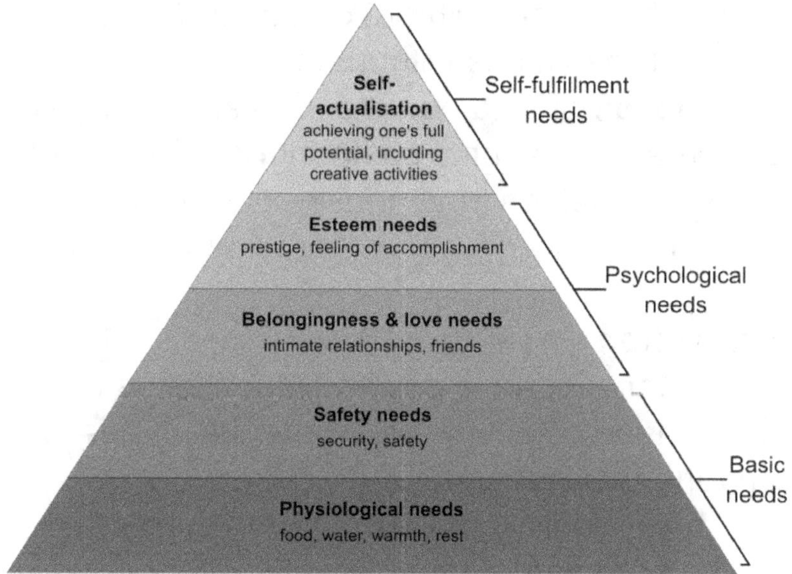

A keen observation gleans ten rudimentary basic needs.
Air, Water, Food, Shelter, Clothes, Fire, Sleep, Defense, Basic first aid and Security
If lost in the wilderness they come in precisely in that order as well.

The rule of threes.
You can survive;
1. Three seconds without presenting your guard or weapon.
2. Three minutes without breathable air.

3. Three hours in a harsh environment.
    (Heat or Cold without protection)
4. Three days without drinkable water.
5. Three weeks without food.

Knowledge of what you need to survive may become an essential component to help you to assess values in your risk and reward planning.

Education

Knowledge is power. Education is the key that unlocks unlimited potential in nearly anyone that pursues it.

The more you learn the more you can learn. Learning is exponential. The more you work on your learning skills the easier it is to learn.

I term it as increasing your rate of assimilation. The more you do, the more you can do.

The more you learn about a particular subject matter the more valuable you become to someone else in the field. The moment you know more about it than most of the people in the room, you become an expert.

Read, study, research, take courses and experiment. Tackle related subjects.

Correspond with people that know more about it than you.

Knowledge is power

Triumph out of adversity
1. Do not turn your current beliefs into a religion.
2. Learn to find inner peace.
3. Do it on purpose.
4. Circumnavigate your anxieties.
5. Be able to stand on your own.
6. Gain self-control.
7. Fortify your integrity.
8. Develop deep relationships and interests.
9. Don't be afraid to take risks.
10. Learn lessons from every setback.

Research

Getting enough information to make an informed decision.

Can you jump over this box?

It's a nice sunny seventy-degree spring day. The box is red and six inches tall. The box is only two feet wide. You get a running start of ten feet.

What questions should you ask?

Wait, is there enough information? You only gave them two dimensions of a 3-D object.

Although you know it's sunny and seventy degrees, this information is irrelevant to your task.

There's a moment of truth (MOT) in every decision.

A moment of truth is simply any interaction during which a customer may form an impression of your brand or product. This impression may be either positive or negative.

If you don't give them enough information it may have a negative effect on your intended accomplishment.

Make it as simple as you can. Too much information may be confusing. Be as straight forward and clear as possible.

No matter how idiot proof you make it, inevitably some idiot will prove you weren't clear enough.

Society

Just like the single cell being in the beginning of life on our planet, society's start out relatively simple.

The first goal is to be able to provide sustenance for one's self and next to your family. Families tend to stick together and support one another. Families tend to have to develop many skills to remain self-sufficient.

Some till, plant and harvest. Others take care of the animals. Some will become a seamstress, cook, housekeeper, laundry detail and so on. Some are mechanics some carpenters until they can maintain a family unit with little or no help from outside influences.

As the society grows in size family units become more specific in nature and experts emerge in a multitude of disciplines.

As the community grows folks lose many skills. Because they now have elevated themselves to a level to be able to afford to hire people to do things for them. In retrospect they even lose the desire to perform those functions.

Then one day their world collapses. Say they lose their job or the economy slows to nearly a stand still. They now are left high and dry with virtually little or no skills at all when it comes to being able to fend for themselves.

Time Management

Identifying productive moments and time wasters. The A, B, C's of your day, week and month.

Try this, it's simple, easy and a good place to start.

Mapping and managing your daily routine.

Take a pad and pen or pencil and make three columns. Make the first one about four or five inches wide and label it, "Events". Make second column about an inch wide and label it, "Time". The third about an inch wide labeled "ABC".

Start the next day. Write down that you wake up and what you do. I. E. Shower, Make the bed, Breakfast, Coffee, Get dressed etc. In the time column, jot down what time you started and time you finished. In the third column score these functions with an "A" for best, "B" for mediocre and "C" for poor use of time.

In this case I would start with an A seeing as you woke up to begin with is a good sign. Next; your trip to work or if you work from home, booting up your computer or getting materials ready to begin a productive day.

Make "Time", start to finish and A, B or C. Continue this throughout your day and on through your entire week. Be as detailed as you'd like. Remember paper is inexpensive and wasted time is not.

If standing around the water dispenser and chatting is productive mark it appropriately.

• Map your day;

Although you can buy a Day Planner it's easy enough to make your own on your computer.

Why is it important you keep track of your daily activities? I want you to ask yourself, when you get to work or school what is the first thing you do? You'll learn how you spend your time and be able to assess how efficient and effectively you utilize the allotted amount of time you have in your day.

Make time? Can we make time? No, of course not, I don't think God will let you or at least our solar system won't. We need to take time. There's 24 hours in a day and that's all you get so it's imperative we all use it wisely.

My dad used to tell me "If you can't get it done in a 24-hour day, you'll have to start working nights".

- Identify time wasters

Back to the question of what is the first thing you do when you get to school or work?

Coffee? Is coffee a time waster? It is if you spend several minutes chatting around the water cooler or coffee machine.

We need to get our priorities in order and pay attention to the goals we've set for ourselves and use our time wisely.

- Combat procrastination

Procrastinating is an easy habit to fall into. I was going to join the Procrastinator's Club once but there'll be plenty of time for that next week. I'm pretty sure my name is on the roster because at one time I thought it was a great idea.

One of the reasons we keep track of our time and plan is so we don't fall into this trap.

Quite frankly it's a deep crevasse, maybe even a bottomless pit.

We are all creatures of habit. Once procrastinating becomes a habit it's a difficult one to break. Pay attention to your every move during your day and avoid this habit at all costs because it could cost you your career.

- Improve efficiencies

Now that we are keeping track of our day, identifying time wasters and combating procrastination we can take time to analyze and assess our daily performance and tweak it in order to achieve better work study habits.

This will result in greatly improving your daily outcome. Profound as it may seem, if you eliminate your inefficiencies, you will become more efficient.

- Keep phone log

I suggest everyone keep a phone log if your job involves communicating on the with anyone in order to complete your job successfully.

For instance, it would be a great idea if you are involved in sales. One of the keys to customer satisfaction is providing them with what they want. You don't have to write entire transcripts but simply jot down key words that will remind you of what transpired in the conversation.

How might this relate to your schooling, well if you are doing research to get answers from another student or a professor, you'd be able go back to your notes and resolve any conflict that may arise.

I've saved my neck several times by going back to my notes when a customer would argue, "That's not what I asked for" or "That's not what we discussed".

I would tell them just a minute, then I would go to my phone log and page back to that conversation and state, "On Oct 14th at 10:41 am you stated . . .". Then from key words in my notes I would go into detail about the instructions or requests.

It's a very effective tool and has saved my butt more than once.

- Daily report

At the end of every day, in a separate file, I take about ten minutes to go through my notes and write a condensed summary of the day highlighting important moments, decisions, statements and actions.

Now if there is a conflict in the future you won't have to go through tons of notes. Scanning your summary's, you can pinpoint the day and then if you need more detail you can go to that day's notes.

"Only those who dare to fail greatly can ever achieve greatly."
- Robert F. Kennedy.

Positive Result Communication

- **Visualization**
We are in general visual creatures and it is of the utmost importance we communicate clearly and precisely what it is that needs to be explained.
- **No such picture**
For instance, there is no picture in our minds for the word "No". No, nearly always has a negative connotation that makes us feel uncomfortable.
You never liked hearing it when you were growing up and that kind of disappointment is a stigma that stays with on into our adulthood. When you asked if you could stay out late that night or for that new

Nintendo and your parents told you, no, it just didn't set right with your desires.

Your folks may have had a real good reason for telling you no but they just left it at no. If they had said, we are afraid you'd get in trouble or even worse you may get hurt staying out that late. Or we don't have the money for that Nintendo but, if you start doing some extra chores around the house you may be able to save enough to buy it yourself in a few months.

Another example would be telling them, "Don't throw your jacket on the floor", instead of, "When you come in the house, hang up your jacket". Either way you're saying the same thing but it's perceived differently just by the manner in with it is presented.

- **Paint a story in their mind**

I'm going to give you an example of how effective getting your point across by painting a picture story is.

There was a polar bear standing on top of a mountain with skis on. On his paws he had green mittens and was holding ski poles. He had a red stocking cap on with a white tassel on top and there was a red and orange striped scarf wrapped around his neck.

- **Be a good listener**
  If you make the conversation about them as often as you can the individual will respond far more positively than if the conversation is about you.

- **Question**
  Asking the right questions nearly always leads them to talk about themselves. People like to talk about themselves in that it's a subject matter that they're familiar with.

- **Pace**
  Match the pace of the conversation as close to their pace as you can. If they talk slow, you should talk slow as well and if they are fast paced pick up the speed and hang in there with them.

- **Mirror**
  Mirror their actions as best as you can. If they lean forward with their elbows on the table do the same. If they lean back in their chair and cross their legs mirror that action

and it nearly always results in them feeling more comfortable. If they're at home with your conversation they are more apt to tune into what you're trying to tell them.

The Art of Persuasion

Construct questions that get results

If you construct your questioning in a proper manner it will result in you controlling the conversation.

Getting it to be their idea

The ability to persuade or convince someone to do anything that benefits yourself is a skill that is unwittingly developed at a very early age.

Procedure; How to convince someone.

Now or Never Close

Creating a sense of urgency prompting an immediate sale such as; this is the last one or we can get you into this one today for 20% off.

Summary Close

Developing a list of benefits emphasizing the value of the agreed upon points by getting them to visualize what they are going to achieve by moving forward with their purchase.

Sharp Angle Close

When a prospective client asks for something extra to be added or a price reduction. You take them by surprise by stating; Sure, then you'll take it with you today?

Question Close

By asking the potential buyer the right series of questions one can eliminate any objections while gaining a commitment to the purchase at the same time. Questions like; does this solve your problem? Or is there any reason we shouldn't move forward with the delivery at this time? Ask for more information and when your certain it's a win-win situation, ask for the sale.

Assumption Close

If you're convinced the sale is going to happen now. Monitor the buyer's commitment and move ahead asking. Does everything we presented meet your expectations? Does this product fit your needs? Would this be a value to your situation? If you assume good intent from the start you'll come off as confident and closing should be easier.

The Takeaway Close

One of the most substantial motivators is the sense of loss even to the extent of losing something you perceived going to already obtained. It's usually a risky tactic frequently utilized to determine whether a fence sitting individual is serious about making the commitment or not. If a potential buyer is undecided it will usually get them to make a decision or move on.

Soft Close

If our product will make them a hero at home or the workplace, point out how. This will save you 20% of the time it takes now and costs less to maintain. This gives you more time to decipher what other needs or objections they have.

Asking for more than you expect

The problem of asking for too much is you may have to settle for nothing. On the other hand, asking for too little and receiving it leaves you with having to find somewhere else to make up the difference to supply your needs. Or to have to get by with an insufficient quantity of what qualifies in order to finish the job.

This is usually not nearly as satisfying as getting the exact amount or more than what you need.

Buying Signals
- If they look genuinely interested.
- Stop your presentation to ask questions.
- If they tell you about their needs.
- If they provide information pertaining to issues about current solution.

Validation (inquisitive statement)
Always validate their response with a statement-question.

So, you want the added features, right?

This looks like something you'd like, right?

That is a program you'd benefit from, correct?

We can move forward with this plan, alright?

This program will save you money, correct?

This would your company, understand?

You'd look great then, wouldn't you?

Try to never say anything negative.
Point - Counter Point.

Have a back-up bag of information.

Always have an answer to anything they could ask. Write down all possible objections and construct responses. Practice your answers in the mirror. If you bring up something you have no answer for, make note of it and formulate a response in case it ever happens again.

Avoid politics and religion.

Company Cultures are Subjective

Just like companies, individuals have an internal culture. It's plainly the way they see things.

Having never been beyond the constraints of what they've learn up until now, they have a difficult time envisioning anything other than that.

It's the way I've/we've done it. Why change?

This has always worked for us/me. These are habits, some good and some bad. Changing habits is one of the most difficult tasks I've run across. Remember changing your own habits is hard, so you have to have a really good plan in order to change someone else's.

Luck

Does luck have anything to do with success? Of course, there is a modicum of luck in everything we do however, there's also a moment of truth in every decision and timing has a lot to do with it.

Root Cause Analysis

In science and engineering, root cause analysis is a method of problem solving used for identifying the root causes of faults or problems. It is widely used in IT operations, telecommunications, industrial process control, accident analysis, medicine, healthcare industry, etc. <u>Wikipedia</u>

Three Moments of Truth

1. The First Moment of Truth is when the customer sees the brand or product,
2. The Second Moment of Truth is when the customer uses, agrees with or coincides with the brand or product.

3. The Third Moment of Truth is when the customer gives an opinion or feedback about the brand and or product.

Problem Solving
Identify what the problem is
Pareto's Law or the 80/20 principal.

In 1906, Italian economist Vilfredo Pareto created a mathematical formula to describe the unequal distribution of wealth in his country, observing that twenty percent of the people owned eighty percent of the wealth.

In the late 1940s, Dr. Joseph M. Juran inaccurately attributed the 80/20 Rule to Pareto, calling it Pareto's Principle. While it may be misnamed, Pareto's Principle or Pareto's Law as it is sometimes called, can be a very effective tool to help you manage effectively. As a result, Dr. Juran's observation of the "vital few and trivial many", the principle that 20 percent of something always are responsible for 80 percent of the results, became known as Pareto's Principle or the 80/20 Rule.

What It Means

The 80/20 Rule means that in anything a few (20 percent) are vital and many (80 percent) are trivial. In Pareto's case it meant 20 percent of the people owned 80 percent of the wealth.

In Juran's initial work he identified 20 percent of the defects causing 80 percent of the problems. Project Managers know that 20 percent of the work (the first 10 percent and the last 10 percent) consume 80 percent of your time and resources. You can apply the 80/20 Rule to almost anything, from the science of management to the physical world.

You know 20 percent of your stock takes up 80 percent of your warehouse space and that 80 percent of your stock comes from 20 percent of your suppliers. Also, 80 percent of your sales will come from 20 percent of your sales staff. 20 percent of your staff will cause 80 percent of your problems, but another 20 percent of your staff will provide 80 percent of your production. It works both ways.

Look for the root cause. Using the 5 W's Ask; Who, What, Where, When and Why.

Use the 5 whys; The answer to simply asking why once generally doesn't clarify the problem thoroughly enough to solve it.

Example:

It was too big.

1. Why was that a problem?
2. Why was it too big? The customer's request wasn't clear enough.
3. Why wasn't the customer's request clear enough? We didn't ask about size.
4. Why didn't we ask about size? It was never a problem in the past.
5. Why was it never a problem in the past? It had met or exceeded all of our customers' needs in the past.

As you can see asking why several times uncovered a host of potential problems to be solved.

Once you have identified the problem and or problems it's time to move on to the next step.

Make a plan

After identifying what is perceived to be the root cause or causes make a list of ways you can resolve the problem or problems.

There is always more than one way to correct the problematic situation.

Analyze each way and choose the best way and if it doesn't work try the next best way.

Use "Uncommon Sense" in that common sense is more than likely one of the causes for getting into the problematic situation in the first place.

Act

- From the plan you've made, take step by step actions to remedy the problem that arose.

Repeat

- Repeat the entire process to make sure there isn't an underlying problem that wasn't detected the first go around.

Remember if you remove everything that can go wrong the only thing left is for things to go right.

Sustain

- Now that you've done the best to resolve all issues make sure there's a method to be able to maintain the status quo. One way to assure you don't back slide into the same problem is to go back through notes you've taken in order to resolve the issue and periodically review it to make sure you are still on track.

Constructing Positive Relationships

- Contacts
Just as we talked about earlier, emulating ones you admire or ones that have achieved the same goals that you've set forth for yourself is a good first step.

If you hang with losers, what do you think the outcome will be? Yep, you more than likely you will achieve that same status.

So, I'm suggesting you hang around with successful professionals and people with goals of good intent.

Those who strive to better themselves every day. It's a good idea to develop a list of an idea a day that will bring you one step closer to excellence and one step closer to achieving your ultimate goal.

Outward Presentation
- Confidence building
Your outward appearance is an important step in your success. Dress for success. Make sure you look good. Eat

healthy and exercise. Hygiene and proper hydration will keep you in the pink.

Remember all things in moderation, including moderation. In other words, go out and get wild once in a while but don't make anything an unhealthy habit. Bottom line if you feel good, you'll look good.

- Promote yourself

If you construct positive relationships with, you're more likely to attain a position in the profession you desire. Take every opportunity to place yourself in the lime light.

If there's an organization you can join; do it. If there are publicly held conventions or meeting that you can attend, be there, bump elbows with those professionals that you want to be like.

If you accomplish some noteworthy achievement in the realm of your interests let local and national publications become aware of what and/or where it happened and what significant it has. See if you can get it in the local newspaper and/or larger trade magazines.

Inner Perspective
- Self esteem

Make sure you make the right decisions in your life. No one is perfect and you will make mistakes but, don't worry about it. Try again.

Albert Einstein said, "Anyone who has never made a mistake has never tried anything new". And the definition of **Insanity**: "doing the same thing over and over again and expecting different results. And Albert Einstein was a pretty smart man, right?

• Move away from negativity
What is the definition of redundant?

Mark Twain said, "Say you're an idiot and then say you're a member of congress".

The definition actually means; superfluous, able to be cut out, which in this case we'd all wish they cut idiots out from congress but who'd run the country?

If there are negative people or circumstances in your presences, walk away.

Although it's not always possible avoid putting yourself in those types of situations.

There was a department in a company I was running that was a disappointment and I wished I could just have them go away.

Then it dawned on me, if I was to take all the people in the world that I thought were dumber than I and eliminate them, I would be the dumbest one in the world.

On the flip side of that if I eliminated everyone, I thought was smarter than I, there would be a lot of people left but I would be the smartest one on the planet and we would all be doomed.

So, thank goodness we are not all equal. We need leaders and followers alike.

Move toward positive things. Surround yourself with positive people and positive events.

"Your mind is a powerful thing. When you fill it with positive thoughts your life will start to change". Zig Ziglar

Although a lot of things I've tried didn't turn out the way I anticipated or planned I've been a success at everything I've ever attempted because through some of them I learned very valuable lessons.

Read body language.

Observe, like a top notch "A1" detective. Know your surroundings if you're in a job interview or at someone's house. Take a look at their furnishings and be able to perceive their Likes and Dislikes. Visual, Listening, Key in on their interests.

Self-sufficiency is one key to success.

Unknown origin

Grandmother says... Carrots, Eggs, or Coffee; "Which are you?"

A young woman went to her grandmother and told her about her life and how things were so hard for her. She did not know how she was going to make it and wanted to give up.

She was tired of fighting and struggling. It seemed as one problem was solved a new one arose.

Her grandmother took her to the kitchen. She filled three pots with water.

In the first, she placed carrots, in the second she placed eggs and the last she placed ground coffee beans.

She let them sit and boil without saying a word.

In about twenty minutes she turned off the burners. She fished the carrots out and placed them in a bowl. She pulled the eggs out and placed them in a bowl. Then she ladled the coffee out and placed it in a bowl.

Turning to her granddaughter, she asked, "Tell me what do you see?"

"Carrots, eggs, and coffee," she replied.

She brought her closer and asked her to feel the carrots. She did and noted that they got soft. She then asked her to take an egg and break it.

After pulling off the shell, she observed the hard-boiled egg.

Finally, she asked her to sip the coffee. The granddaughter smiled, as she tasted its rich aroma.

The granddaughter then asked. "What's the point, grandmother?"

Her grandmother explained that each of these objects had faced the same adversity-- boiling water--but each reacted differently.

The carrot went in strong, hard and unrelenting. However, after being subjected to the boiling water, it softened and became weak.

The egg had been fragile. Its thin outer shell had protected its liquid interior. But, after sitting through the boiling water, its inside became hardened.

The ground coffee beans were unique, however. After they were in the boiling water, they had changed the water.

"Which are you?" she asked her granddaughter.

"When adversity knocks on your door, how do you respond? Are you a carrot, an egg, or a coffee bean?"

Think of this: Which am I?

Am I the carrot that seems strong, but with pain and adversity, do I wilt and become soft and lose my strength?

Am I the egg that starts with a malleable heart, but changes with the heat? Did I have a fluid spirit, but after a death, a breakup, a financial hardship or some other trial, have I become hardened and stiff?

Does my shell look the same, but on the inside am I bitter and tough with a stiff spirit and a hardened heart?

Or am I like the coffee bean? The bean actually changes the hot water, the very circumstance that brings the pain. When the water gets hot, it releases the fragrance and flavor.

If you are like the bean, when things are at their worst, you get better and change the situation around you.

When the hours are the darkest and trials are their greatest do you elevate to another level?

I do have the things God gifted me with and one of those is my short-comings.

I was born with the gifts that God gave me and if short comings are my long suit, what should I do.

The benefits of following the hand full of guidelines I've laid out for you today is, it will set you in a mode of continual improvement. We should all strive to be a better person every day.

You can do it. All you have to do is apply yourself, try and you will achieve your goal.

My father used to tell me, "There is no easy way to do hard work because, if there was everybody would be doing something that's easy and nobody's going to pay you the big bucks for doing something that's easy".

I had a boss that told me once; "There's no "I" in team" And I replied, "but there are two in "Idiot".

Dwight D. Eisenhauer
"What is important is rarely urgent, what is urgent is rarely important."

Sod's Second Law
Sooner or later, the worst possible set of circumstances is bound to occur.
Corollary Any system must be designed to withstand the worst possible set of circumstances.

Fudd's First Law of Relativity
If it's possible to push something hard enough.
Corollary It will fall over.

TPS is an integrated socio-technical system, developed by Toyota, that comprises its management philosophy and practices. The TPS is a management system that organizes manufacturing and logistics for the automobile manufacturer, including interaction with suppliers and customers. The system is a major precursor of the more generic "lean manufacturing". <u>Taiichi Ohno</u> and <u>Eiji Toyoda</u>, Japanese industrial engineers, developed the system between 1948 and 1975.[2]

Originally called "<u>just-in-time production</u>", it builds on the approach created by the founder of Toyota, <u>Sakichi Toyoda</u>, his son <u>Kiichiro Toyoda</u>, and the engineer <u>Taiichi Ohno</u>.

Six Sigma is a set of techniques and tools for process improvement. It was introduced by

Sigma Level	Defects per Million	Yield
6	3.4	99.99966%
5	230	99.977%
4	6,210	99.38%
3	66,800	93.32%
2	308,000	69.15%
1	690,000	30.85%

American engineer <u>Bill Smith</u> while working at <u>Motorola</u> in 1986.[1][2] A six sigma process is one in which 99.99966% of all opportunities to produce some feature of a part are statistically expected to be free of defects.

"Everything in moderation including moderation" Oscar Wilde was an Irish poet and playwright. After writing in different forms throughout the 1880s, he became one of the most popular playwrights in London in the early 1890s.

Why is DMAIC important?

DMAIC is a structured, data-driven methodology used in Six Sigma for process improvement. It consists of five phases:

1. **Define**: Identify the problem, project goals, and requirements. Establish the scope and create a clear problem statement.
2. **Measure**: Collect data to understand the current process performance. Establish baseline metrics and assess the process capability.
3. **Analyze**: Identify root causes of the problem using data analysis tools. Pinpoint factors contributing to defects or inefficiencies.
4. **Improve**: Develop and implement solutions to address root causes. Test improvements through pilots, refine them, and optimize the process.
5. **Control**: Monitor the improved process to sustain results. Implement controls like standard operating procedures and

statistical process control to prevent
regression.
DMAIC is widely used to reduce defects,
improve quality, and enhance efficiency in
processes.

The **5 Whys** is a problem-solving technique
used to identify the root cause of an issue by
repeatedly asking "Why?"—typically five
times—until the underlying cause is revealed.
It's often used within the **Analyze** phase of the
DMAIC methodology to dig deeper into the
reasons behind a problem.
How It Works:
1. **State the Problem**: Clearly define the
   issue you're addressing.
2. **Ask "Why?"**: Ask why the problem is
   occurring and provide a specific answer.
3. **Repeat**: Use the answer as the basis for
   the next "Why?" question. Continue asking
   "Why?" (usually five times, though it can be
   more or fewer) until the root cause is
   identified.
4. **Validate the Root Cause**: Ensure the
   identified cause is actionable and
   addresses the problem effectively.
5. **Develop Solutions**: Create
   countermeasures to address the root
   cause and prevent recurrence.

Key Points:
- **Simplicity**: It's straightforward and requires no complex tools.
- **Depth**: Encourages digging beyond symptoms to find the true cause.
- **Flexibility**: Can stop at fewer or continue past five "Whys" if needed.
- **Limitations**: Effectiveness depends on the quality of answers and may miss multiple contributing causes if not combined with other tools.

The 5 Whys is widely used in Lean, Six Sigma, and other process improvement frameworks to drive corrective actions and prevent problem recurrence.

The 5W Framework

The 5W framework is a method to gather comprehensive information about a situation, problem, or event by answering five key questions. It's useful in the **Define** phase of DMAIC to scope a problem or in root cause analysis alongside tools like the **5 Whys**.

Who:

Identifies the people involved or affected. Example: Who is experiencing the problem? Who is responsible for the process?

In DMAIC: Defines stakeholders, customers, or team members.

What:

Describes the problem, event, or process in detail.

Example: What is the specific issue? What is the desired outcome?

In DMAIC: Clarifies the problem statement or goal.

Where:

Specifies the location or context of the issue.

Example: Where does the problem occur (e.g., department, facility)?

In DMAIC: Narrows the scope to a specific process or area.

When:

Determines the timing or frequency of the issue.

Example: When does the problem occur (e.g., specific times, shifts)?

In DMAIC: Helps establish a timeline for data collection or problem occurrence.

Why:

Explores the reasons or causes behind the issue.

Example: Why is this happening? (This can lead into the **5 Whys** technique.)

In DMAIC: Sets the stage for root cause analysis in the **Analyze** phase.

Relation to 5 Whys and DMAIC

The **5W** framework is broader and helps define the problem comprehensively, often in the **Define** phase of DMAIC. It ensures all aspects of the issue are understood before diving into solutions.

The **5 Whys**, used in the **Analyze** phase, focuses specifically on the "Why" component, drilling down to the root cause of the problem identified in the 5W analysis.

Example in DMAIC:

Define (5W): The machine stops frequently (What), in the production line (Where), during night shifts (When), affecting operators (Who). Why? Initial answer: fuse issues.

Analyze (5 Whys): Why does the fuse blow? Overload. Why overload? Machine runs beyond capacity. Why? Operator error. Why? No training. Why? No training programs. **Root Cause**: Lack of training.

Example Application

Problem: Customer complaints about late deliveries.

1. **Who**: Customers, delivery team.
2. **What**: Orders are delivered late.
3. **Where**: Distribution center.

4. **When**: During peak holiday seasons.
5. **Why**: Initial reason—inefficient scheduling. (Leads to 5 Whys: Why inefficient? Overloaded trucks. Why? Poor forecasting. Why? No demand analysis. Why? Lack of tools. Why? No budget allocated. **Root Cause**: No budget for demand forecasting tools.)

Key Points

Comprehensive: Ensures a holistic understanding of the problem.

Versatile: Used in journalism, project management, Six Sigma, and more.

Complementary: Pairs well with **5 Whys** for root cause analysis or DMAIC for process improvement.

Actionable: Helps structure data collection and problem-solving.

Good Questions are the Answer.

Asking "Why" questions is a powerful technique for uncovering deeper insights, identifying root causes, and generating meaningful answers. Here's why they are so effective, particularly in problem-solving contexts like DMAIC or the 5 Whys:

1. **Drives to Root Causes**:
   "Why" questions peel back layers of symptoms to reveal the underlying

reasons for a problem. Instead of addressing superficial issues, they help pinpoint the core cause, leading to more effective solutions.

2. **Encourages Critical Thinking**: "Why" prompts reflection and analysis, forcing you to challenge assumptions and think beyond the obvious. This leads to more thoughtful, well-rounded answers.

3. **Uncovers Hidden Connections**: By repeatedly asking "Why," you connect seemingly unrelated factors, revealing patterns or systemic issues. This holistic view leads to comprehensive solutions.

4. **Promotes Clarity and Specificity**: "Why" questions demand precise answers, reducing vagueness. They push for evidence-based reasoning, ensuring answers are grounded in facts rather than guesses.
Example: "Why is the process slow?" requires data (e.g., bottlenecks at step X due to manual input), leading to targeted improvements.

5. **Sparks Curiosity and Exploration**: "Why" fosters a mindset of inquiry, encouraging exploration of new

perspectives or possibilities. This can uncover innovative solutions or opportunities for improvement.
6. **Facilitates Collaboration**: In team settings, "Why" questions stimulate discussion, drawing out diverse viewpoints and expertise. This collaborative approach yields richer, more actionable answers.

Why It Works in DMAIC and 5 Whys

In **DMAIC**, "Why" questions are central to the **Analyze** phase, where tools like the **5 Whys** systematically drill down to root causes. They ensure solutions address the true problem, not just symptoms, improving process efficiency and quality.

The **5 Whys** leverages "Why" to create a chain of cause-and-effect reasoning, making it simple yet profound for identifying actionable fixes.

Caveats

Quality Matters: Vague or poorly framed "Why" questions can lead to incomplete answers. Specificity is key (e.g., "Why are deliveries late?" vs. "Why is truck scheduling delayed on Mondays?").

Multiple Causes: A single "Why" chain may miss contributing factors. Combining with tools like fishbone diagrams ensures broader coverage.

Resistance: Overuse or aggressive "Why" questioning can feel confrontational. Phrasing and context matter in collaborative settings.

Conclusion

"Why" questions get good answers because they dig beneath the surface, challenge assumptions, and drive clarity, critical thinking, and actionable insights. In frameworks like DMAIC or the 5 Whys, they systematically guide you to root causes, ensuring solutions are effective and sustainable. To maximize their impact, ask "Why" with precision and complement it with other analytical tools when needed.

Why are questions the answer?

Asking questions helps me understand your needs, clarify your intent, and uncover context that might not be immediately obvious. It allows me to gather specific details, refine my responses, and ensure I'm addressing what matters most to you. Insight comes from piecing together your input, my knowledge, and the patterns or gaps I notice through questioning.

Priority Check list

1. **List All Tasks**: Write down every item on your checklist.
2. **Assess Urgency and Importance**: Use the **Eisenhower Matrix** or the **Ben Franklin Analysis**
   Urgent and Important: Do these first (e.g., deadlines today).
   Important but Not Urgent: Schedule these next (e.g., long-term projects).
   Urgent but Not Important: Delegate if possible (e.g., minor interruptions).
   Neither Urgent nor Important: Eliminate or do last (e.g., low-value tasks).
3. **Consider Deadlines**: Rank tasks with fixed due dates higher.
4. **Evaluate Impact**: Prioritize tasks with the biggest outcomes (e.g., high ROI or critical goals).
5. **Estimate Effort**: Balance quick wins (low effort, high impact) with larger tasks.
6. **Reorganize the List**: Number tasks in order of priority.
7. **Review and Adjust**: Reassess as new tasks or changes arise.

The Eisenhower Matrix

The **Eisenhower Matrix**, also known as the **Urgent-Important Matrix**, is a time management and prioritization tool that helps you categorize tasks based on their **urgency** and **importance**. Named after President Dwight D. Eisenhower, who used this approach to manage his workload, it organizes tasks into four quadrants to guide decisions on what to do, schedule, delegate, or eliminate.

How It Works:

Tasks are sorted into a 2x2 grid based on two criteria:

Urgent: Tasks requiring immediate attention (e.g., deadlines, crises).

Important: Tasks that contribute to long-term goals or values (e.g., strategic planning, personal growth).

The Four Quadrants:

Quadrant 1: Urgent and Important (Do First)
Tasks that are both time-sensitive and critical.
Examples: Pressing deadlines, emergencies, critical project deliverables.

Action: Handle these immediately.

Quadrant 2: Important but Not Urgent (Schedule)

Tasks that matter for long-term success but lack immediate deadlines.

Examples: Planning, relationship-building, skill development, exercise.

Action: Plan and schedule these to ensure they're not neglected.

Quadrant 3: Urgent but Not Important (Delegate)

Tasks that demand attention but don't align with your core goals.

Examples: Interruptions, some emails, minor requests from others.

Action: Delegate to others or minimize time spent on these.

Quadrant 4: Neither Urgent nor Important (Eliminate)

Low-value tasks that waste time and don't contribute to goals.

Examples: Mindless scrolling, unnecessary meetings, trivial distractions.

Action: Eliminate or avoid these to free up time.

How to Use It:

List Tasks: Write down all tasks or items from your checklist.

Categorize:

Ask: *Is this task urgent?* (Does it need to be done soon?)

Ask: *Is this task important?* (Does it align with my goals?)
Place each task in the appropriate quadrant.
Take Action:
Tackle Quadrant 1 tasks immediately.
Schedule Quadrant 2 tasks for focused work.
Delegate Quadrant 3 tasks to others if possible.
Eliminate Quadrant 4 tasks to reduce clutter.
Review Regularly: Reassess tasks as priorities shift.
Example:
Checklist: Respond to emails, finish a report due today, exercise, browse social media, attend a low-priority meeting.
Q1 (Do First): Finish report (urgent, important).
Q2 (Schedule): Exercise (important, not urgent).
Q3 (Delegate): Respond to non-critical emails, low-priority meeting (urgent, not important).
Q4 (Eliminate): Browse social media (neither urgent nor important).
Benefits:
Clarifies Priorities: Focuses on what truly matters.
Reduces Stress: Helps manage urgent tasks while preventing neglect of important ones.

Boosts Productivity: Minimizes time on low-value activities.

Tips:

Spend most of your time in **Quadrant 2** to prevent tasks from becoming urgent (proactive work).

Use tools like to-do apps or a simple 2x2 grid on paper to visualize.

Combine with the **Ben Franklin Analysis** for decisions within tasks (e.g., weighing pros and cons of a Quadrant 2 project).

The Ben Franklin Analysis

The **Ben Franklin Analysis**, also known as the **Pros and Cons List** or **Franklin's Decision-Making Method**, is a simple decision-making tool attributed to Benjamin Franklin. It involves weighing the advantages and disadvantages of a decision to make a more informed choice. Franklin described this method in a 1772 letter to Joseph Priestley, explaining how he balanced competing factors to resolve indecision.

How It Works:

Define the Decision: Clearly state the choice or problem (e.g., "Should I take a new job?").

Draw a Two-Column Table:

Label one column **Pros** (benefits, advantages).

Label the other **Cons** (drawbacks, risks).

List All Factors:

Write down all the positive aspects of the decision in the Pros column.

Write down all the negative aspects in the Cons column.

Assign Weights (Optional):

Franklin suggested estimating the relative importance of each pro and con. For example, if one pro is twice as important as a con, it might "cancel out" two cons.

You can assign numerical values (e.g., 1 to 5) to reflect significance.

Balance the Sides:

Compare the lists. Franklin would mentally "strike out" pros and cons of equal weight to see which side had more remaining.

If using numbers, sum the scores for Pros and Cons to see which is higher.

Reflect and Decide: Use the analysis to guide your decision, considering both the quantity and quality of the factors.

Example:

Decision: Should I move to a new city?

Pros:
Better job opportunities (Weight: 4)
Vibrant cultural scene (Weight: 3)
Closer to family (Weight: 2)
Cons:
Higher cost of living (Weight: 4)
Leaving friends behind (Weight: 3)
Moving expenses (Weight: 2)
Analysis: If pros total 9 points and cons total 9, it's a close call. You might prioritize based on which factors (e.g., job opportunities vs. cost of living) matter most to you.
Franklin's Insight:
In his letter, Franklin noted that this method helps clarify trade-offs by laying out all considerations visually. He acknowledged it's not purely mathematical, as judgment still plays a role in weighting factors.
Tips for Use:
Be thorough in listing all relevant pros and cons.
Consider short-term vs. long-term impacts.
Combine with other tools like the Eisenhower Matrix for prioritizing tasks or decisions.
Use for personal decisions (e.g., career moves) or group choices (e.g., business investments).

Merit (Sanskrit: *puṇya*, Pali: *puñña*) is a concept considered fundamental to Buddhist ethics. It is a beneficial and protective force which accumulates as a result of good deeds, acts, or thoughts. **Merit-making** is important to Buddhist practice: merit brings good and agreeable results, determines the quality of the next life and contributes to a person's growth towards enlightenment. In addition, merit is also shared with a deceased loved one, in order to help the deceased in their new existence. Despite modernization, merit-making remains essential in traditional Buddhist countries and has had a significant impact on the rural economies in these countries.

Merit is connected with the notions of purity and goodness. Before Buddhism, merit was used with regard to ancestor worship, but in Buddhism it gained a more general ethical meaning. Merit is a force that results from good deeds done; it is capable of attracting good circumstances in a person's life, as well as improving the person's mind and inner well-being. Moreover, it affects the next lives to come, as well as the destination a person is reborn. The opposite of merit is demerit (*papa*), and it is believed that merit is able to weaken demerit. Indeed, merit has even been connected to the path to <u>Nirvana</u> itself, but many scholars say that this refers only to some types of merit.

Merit can be gained in a number of ways, such as <u>giving</u>, <u>virtue</u> and <u>mental development</u>. In addition, there are many forms of merit-making described in <u>ancient Buddhist texts</u>. A similar concept of *kusala (Sanskrit: kusala)* is also known, which is different from merit in some details. The most fruitful form of merit-making is those good deeds done with regard to the <u>Triple Gem</u>, that is, the <u>Buddha</u>, his teachings, the <u>Dhamma</u> (*Sanskrit: Dharma*), and the <u>Sangha</u>. In Buddhist societies, a great variety of practices involving merit-making has grown throughout the centuries, sometimes involving great self-sacrifice. Merit has become part of <u>rituals</u>, <u>daily and weekly practice</u>, and <u>festivals</u>. In addition, there is a widespread custom of <u>transferring merit</u> to one's deceased relatives, of which the origin is still a matter of scholarly debate. Merit has been that important in Buddhist societies, that <u>kingship</u> was often <u>legitimated</u> through it, and still is.

Murphy's Law ("If anything can go wrong, it will") was born at Edwards Air Force Base in 1949 at North Base.

It was named after Capt. Edward A. Murphy, an engineer working on Air Force Project MX981, (a project) designed to see how much sudden deceleration a person can stand in a crash.
One day, after finding that a transducer was wired wrong, he cursed the technician responsible and said, "If there is any way to do it wrong, he'll find it."

The contractor's project manager kept a list of "laws" and added this one, which he called Murphy's Law.

Airforce

Sod's law, a British culture axiom, states that "if something *can* go wrong, it will". The law sometimes has a corollary: that the misfortune will happen at "the worst possible time" (Finagle's law). The term is commonly used in the United Kingdom, though in North America, the phrase "Murphy's law" is more popular.[1]

The phrase seems to derive, at least in part, from the colloquialism an "unlucky sod"; a term for someone who has had some bad (unlucky) experience, and is usually used as a sympathetic reference to the person.[2]

A slightly different form of Sod's law states that "the degree of failure is in direct proportion to the effort expended and to the need for success."[3]

An alternative expression, again in British culture, is "hope for the best, expect the worst".[4]

Barriers

Overcoming barriers to meritocracy requires addressing systemic, structural, and individual obstacles that prevent talent, effort, and achievement from being fairly recognized and rewarded. A true meritocracy ensures that everyone has an equal opportunity to compete based on their abilities and hard work, regardless of background, privilege, or circumstances.

I will explain in-depth common barriers to meritocracy and practical strategies to overcome them, organized by key areas: access to opportunity, bias and discrimination, resource inequality, measurement of merit, and cultural/institutional resistance.

The journey to a true meritocracy is ongoing, but every step—whether it's a scholarship for a deserving student, a blind hiring process, or a policy reform—moves us closer to a world where everyone has a fair shot to earn their place.

1. Barrier: Limited Access to Opportunity
Description: Meritocracy assumes everyone has a fair shot, but unequal access to education, networks, or opportunities can prevent talented individuals from even entering the competition. For example, a brilliant student from a low-income area may lack access to quality schools or mentorship, limiting their ability to showcase their merit.
Strategies to Overcome:
- **Expand Access to Education**: Invest in public education, particularly in underserved communities, to ensure all students have access to quality teachers, curricula, and resources. Programs like scholarships, free online courses (e.g., Khan Academy), or community-based tutoring can bridge gaps.
- **Create Mentorship Programs**: Pair individuals from underrepresented backgrounds with mentors who can

provide guidance, networks, and insider knowledge. For instance, organizations like Big Brothers Big Sisters or industry-specific mentorship initiatives can open doors.

- **Promote Early Exposure**: Introduce young people to diverse career paths through internships, job shadowing, or STEM camps. Programs like Girls Who Code expose underrepresented groups to fields where they can demonstrate merit.
- **Remove Gatekeeping Barriers**: Simplify application processes for jobs, schools, or grants to reduce hurdles like complex paperwork or insider-only networks. Transparent criteria and outreach to diverse communities help level the playing field.

Example: The Posse Foundation identifies talented students from diverse backgrounds, provides them with leadership training, and places them in supportive cohorts at top universities, ensuring they have the tools to compete on merit.

2. Barrier: Bias and Discrimination

Description: Conscious or unconscious biases—based on race, gender,

socioeconomic status, or other factors—can distort how merit is evaluated. For example, studies show that identical resumes with "white-sounding" names receive more callbacks than those with "ethnic" names, undermining merit-based hiring.
Strategies to Overcome:
- **Implement Blind Evaluations**: Use anonymized processes to assess merit. For example, blind auditions in orchestras (where musicians perform behind a screen) increased the hiring of women by focusing solely on performance.
- **Train for Bias Awareness**: Offer regular training to decision-makers (e.g., hiring managers, admissions officers) on recognizing and mitigating unconscious bias. Tools like implicit bias workshops can improve fairness.
- **Standardize Evaluation Criteria**: Develop clear, objective metrics for assessing merit, such as specific skills, qualifications, or performance outcomes. Rubrics and scorecards reduce subjective judgments that invite bias.
- **Diversify Decision-Making Panels**: Ensure that those evaluating merit come

from varied backgrounds. Diverse perspectives counteract groupthink and reduce the likelihood of bias favoring certain groups.

Example: Companies like Google have adopted structured interviews with standardized questions and scoring to minimize bias, ensuring candidates are judged on skills and accomplishments rather than subjective impressions.

3. Barrier: Resource Inequality

Description: Meritocracy assumes a level playing field, but disparities in wealth, technology, or support systems can hinder individuals' ability to develop or demonstrate their potential. For instance, a low-income worker may lack the time or money to pursue advanced training, even if they have the talent.

Strategies to Overcome:

- **Provide Financial Support**: Offer scholarships, grants, or subsidized training programs to remove financial barriers. Income-based aid, like Pell Grants in the U.S., helps talented students afford higher education.
- **Ensure Access to Technology**: Bridge the digital divide by providing affordable

internet, devices, or public tech hubs. Initiatives like One Laptop Per Child aim to equip underserved communities with tools for learning and skill-building.

- **Offer Flexible Pathways**: Create opportunities that accommodate diverse circumstances, such as part-time training, online certifications, or apprenticeships. These allow individuals to develop skills without sacrificing income or family responsibilities.
- **Support Work-Life Balance**: Provide resources like childcare, mental health support, or flexible work hours to help individuals focus on skill development and performance. This is especially critical for single parents or low-income workers.

Example: The German apprenticeship model combines paid on-the-job training with education, allowing individuals from varied economic backgrounds to gain skills and compete in the job market based on merit.

---

4. Barrier: Flawed Measurement of Merit

Description: Merit is often misjudged due to overly narrow or subjective criteria. For example, standardized tests may favor those with access to expensive prep courses, or "cultural fit" in hiring may prioritize likability over ability, sidelining diverse talent.

Strategies to Overcome:

- **Broaden Definitions of Merit**: Evaluate a wider range of skills and experiences. For instance, in hiring, consider not just formal degrees but also self-taught skills, portfolio projects, or resilience in overcoming adversity.
- **Use Holistic Assessments**: Combine multiple metrics—tests, interviews, work samples, and references—to capture a fuller picture of ability. Universities like MIT use holistic admissions to value creativity and grit alongside academic scores.
- **Validate Alternative Credentials**: Recognize non-traditional qualifications, such as coding bootcamps, micro-credentials, or open-source contributions, which demonstrate merit without requiring expensive degrees.
- **Regularly Audit Evaluation Systems**: Review hiring, promotion, or admissions processes to ensure they reward true merit. Data analysis can reveal patterns (e.g., underrepresentation of certain groups) that signal flaws in measurement.

Example: The software industry increasingly values GitHub portfolios and open-source contributions as proof of coding ability, allowing self-taught developers to compete with those holding formal degrees.

---

5. Barrier: Cultural and Institutional Resistance

Description: Some organizations or societies resist meritocracy due to entrenched traditions, favoritism, or fear of change. For example, legacy admissions in universities or "old boys' networks" in corporations prioritize connections over competence.

Strategies to Overcome:

- **Champion Transparency**: Publicize criteria for decisions like hiring, promotions, or funding. Transparency holds institutions accountable and discourages favoritism. For example, publishing pay scales can expose inequities.
- **Enforce Accountability**: Establish independent oversight, such as ethics boards or ombudsmen, to investigate claims of unfair practices. Whistleblower protections encourage reporting of nepotism or cronyism.

- **Cultivate a Merit-Based Culture**: Leaders should model meritocratic values by rewarding performance and publicly recognizing contributions. This sets a tone that prioritizes results over politics.
- **Advocate for Policy Change**: Push for reforms that dismantle anti-meritocratic practices. For instance, eliminating legacy admissions (as some U.S. colleges have done) ensures spots are earned through achievement.

Example: Norway's corporate board gender quotas, paired with merit-based selection criteria, have increased diversity while maintaining high standards, showing that systemic change can align with meritocracy.

6. Barrier: Lack of Feedback and Growth Opportunities

Description: Without constructive feedback or chances to improve, individuals may struggle to develop the skills needed to demonstrate merit. This is particularly true for those in under-resourced environments or toxic workplaces.

Strategies to Overcome:
- **Provide Constructive Feedback**: Train managers and educators to give

specific, actionable feedback that helps individuals grow. Regular performance reviews can guide skill development.

- **Offer Skill-Building Opportunities**: Create accessible training programs, workshops, or stretch assignments that allow individuals to enhance their abilities. Companies like IBM offer free digital skills courses to employees and the public.
- **Foster Safe Learning Environments**: Encourage risk-taking and experimentation by creating spaces where failure is a learning opportunity, not a career-ender. Psychological safety boosts confidence to pursue merit.
- **Recognize Incremental Progress**: Reward improvement and effort, not just final outcomes. This motivates individuals to keep developing, especially those starting from disadvantaged positions.

Example: The nonprofit Year Up provides young adults from low-income backgrounds with professional training, internships, and feedback, helping them build skills and compete in merit-based job markets.

7. Barrier: Socioeconomic and Systemic Inequities

Description: Deep-rooted societal issues, such as poverty, healthcare disparities, or incarceration rates, can prevent individuals from having the stability or resources to pursue merit-based goals. These systemic inequities create uneven starting points.

Strategies to Overcome:

- **Address Basic Needs**: Support policies and programs that provide healthcare, housing, or food security, enabling individuals to focus on education and career goals. Universal basic income pilots, like those in Finland, have shown promise in stabilizing lives.
- **Reform Criminal Justice Systems**: Reduce barriers for formerly incarcerated individuals by expunging records for minor offenses or offering reentry programs that provide job training. Ban-the-box laws help ex-offenders compete based on merit.
- **Invest in Community Infrastructure**: Build libraries, community centers, or public transportation in underserved areas to give residents access to learning and job opportunities.

- **Advocate for Equitable Policies**:
Support legislation that tackles systemic
inequities, such as fair wages,
affordable childcare, or anti-
discrimination laws, to create conditions
where merit can shine.

Example: The Harlem Children's Zone
provides comprehensive support—education,
health services, and family programs—to
break the cycle of poverty, enabling kids to
pursue merit-based success.

Conclusion

Overcoming barriers to meritocracy
requires a multi-faceted approach that
combines individual empowerment,
institutional reform, and societal change. By
expanding access to opportunities, reducing
bias, addressing resource gaps, refining how
merit is measured, and dismantling cultural
resistance, we can create systems where
talent and effort are the true determinants of
success. These strategies not only benefit
individuals but also strengthen organizations
and societies by ensuring the best ideas and
contributions rise to the top.

Time Sheet

Date _____ **Month**_____ **Year** ___________

6:00 ____

6:30 ____

7:00 ____

7:30 ____

8:00 ____

8:30 ____

9:00 ____

9:30 ____

10:00 ____

10:30 ____

11:00 ____

11:30 ____

12:00 ____

12:30 ____

1:00 ____

1:30 ____

2:00 ____

2:30 ____

3:00 ____

3:30 ____

4:00 ____

4:30 ____

5:00 ____

5:30 ____

Weekly Planner __/__/____

Monday ________________________________

____

____

____

Tuesday ________________________________

____

____

Wednesday ______________________________

____

____

Thursday _______________________________

____

____

Friday _________________________________

____

____

Saturday _______________________________

Sunday _________________________________

Phone Log

Date   **Time**   **Person**

Things To Do

Things That Went Well Today

Time Wasters

Goal of the day ___/___/_____

1. _______________________

____

____

____

2. _______________________

____

____

____

3. _______________________

____

____

____

4. _______________________

____

____

____

The **Pareto Principle**, also known as
the **80/20 Rule**, The Law of the Vital Few and
The **Principle** of Factor Sparsity, illustrates
that 80% of effects arise from 20% of the
causes – or in lamens terms – 20% of your
actions/activities will account for 80% of your
results/outcomes.

The **80/20 productivity rule** is one of them. It
clearly states that 80% of your results come
from 20% of your efforts. This **principle** was
developed by Vilferdo Pareto, an Italian
economist and sociologist who first observed
the **rule** when analyzing wealth and income
distribution trends in Europe.

Applying it to the business world, the **80/20
rule** suggests that 80% of your company
sales come from 20% of your customers.

- 20% of criminals commit 80% of crimes.
- 20% of drivers cause 80% of all traffic
  accidents.
- 80% of pollution originates from 20% of all
  factories.
- 20% of a company's products represent 80%
  of sales.

- 20% of employees are responsible for 80% of the results.
- 20% of students have grades 80% or higher.

The List of Examples

80% of a company's output is produced by 20% of its workers.

80% of social media shares are by 20% of posts.

80% of software glitches are caused by 20% of bugs.

80% of search visits involve 20% of keywords.

80% of promotions are given by 20% of bosses.

80% of budget overruns are caused by 20% of expenses.

80% of your success comes from 20% of your ideas.

80% of the public uses 20% of their computers' features.

80% of crimes are committed by 20% of criminals.

80% of sales are from 20% of clients.

80% of project value is achieved with
the *first* 20% of effort.
80% of your knowledge is used 20% of the
time.
80% of sales are produce by 20% of a
company's products or services.
80% of stress are caused by 20% of
stressors.
80% of rapid promotions are available in 20%
of companies.
80% of value perceived by customers relates
to 20% of what an organization does.
80% of the wealth is owned by 20% of the
population.
80% of negotiation concessions occur in the
last 20% of negotiations.
80% of the population finds only 20% of it
attractive.
80% of sleep quality occurs in 20% of sleep.
80% of results are caused by 20% of thinking
and planning.
80% of family problems are caused by 20%
of issues.
80% of retail sales are produced by 20% of a
store's brands.
80% of website traffic comes from 20% of
content.
80% of opportunity is created by 20% of
instigative impulses.

80% of new customers are generated by 20% of new offerings.
80% of muscle gain is built by 20% of the repetitions.
80% of complaints are by 20% of customers.
80% of a town's traffic are on 20% of its roads.
80% of innovation comes from 20% of the population.
80% of a product's costs involve 20% of its parts.
80% of software functionality are caused by 20% of the software developers' efforts.
80% of news coverage is based on 20% of world events.
80% of inventory comes from 20% of suppliers.
80% of your weekly tasks affect 20% of your future.
80% of grief is caused by 20% of people in your life.
80% of alarm will be set off by 20% of potential causes.
80% of energy in a combustion engine produces 20% output.
80% of people marry within 20% of the local population.
80% of company's absenteeism is caused by 20% of staff.

80% of investment gains are produced by 20% of investments.
80% of the benefit from any product or service can be provided at 20% of cost.
80% of profits made by all industries are made by 20% of industries.
80% of profits made in any industry are made by 20% of firms.
80% of a market is supplied by 20% of suppliers.
80% of projects get completed in the last 20% of time before a deadline.

The Inverse

20% of your wardrobe is worn 80% of the time.
20% of farmers produce 80% of the world's agriculture.
20% of your rug has 80% of the wear-and-tear.
20% of your phone apps get 80% usage.
20% of foods cause 80% of the weight gain.
20% of your TV channels are watched 80% of the time.
20% of the population implement 80% of their creative ideas.
20% of issues represent 80% of the materiality of the negotiations.
20% of your thoughts lead to 80% of ideas.

20% of your allies will help 80% of your success.
20% of companies, which achieved world-class status, outsource 80% of operations.
20% of words in a language accounts for 80% of usage.
20% of laws are broken 80% of the time.
20% of people in your life consume 80% of your time.
20% of planning causes 80% of a project's success.
20% of workers initiate focus on issues that require 80% attention.
20% of your time leads to 80% of your happiness.
20% of work occupations cause 80% of workplace injuries.
20% of cities have 80% of the populations.
20% of your social circle has 80% of its optimism.
20% of shareholders own 80% of a corporation's stock.
20% of a company's inventory consume 80% of the space.
20% of your habits create 80% of your productivity.
20% of the population produce 80% of innovation.

20% of the foods you eat produce 80% of your energy.
20% of people produce 80% of innovation.
20% of cell phone users consumer 80% of wireless bandwidth.
20% of your work tasks produce 80% of results for the day, month, year.
20% of professional athletes cause 80% of ticket sales.
20% of your relationships consumed 80% of your dating life.
20% of your social circle provide you with 80% of the value.
20% of your friends produce 80% of inspiration.
20% of computer bugs fixed will stop 80% of crashes.
20% of the population cause 80% of car crashes.
20% of doctors, lawyers, and engineers commit 80% of malpractice.
20% of your experiences produce 80% of your happiness.
20% of the hours in a workday yield 80% of the productivity.
20% of bar liquor is consumed 80% of the time.
20% of the earth's inhabitants cause 80% of the world's problems.

20% of the population have 80% of qualities you most want in a partner.
20% of companies cause 80% of the pollution.
20% of your project (first 10% and last 10%) will consume 80% of your attention.
20% of work hazards produce 80% of injuries.
20% of efforts in betting matches 80% of the bettors.
20% of patients use 80% of health care resources.
20% of your knowledge is used 80% of the time.
20% of infected humans transmit 80% of the diseases.
20% of clothes packed in a suitcase are worn 80% of the time.
20% of newspapers are viewed 80% of the time.
20% of those who marry cause 80% of divorces.
20% of thieves make off with 80% of the loot.
20% of beer drinkers consume 80% of beer drunk.
20% of investment portfolios produce 80% of the gain.
20% of children will obtain 80% of educational qualifications available.

Key Insights and Takeaways:

•	Life is nonlinear. Forces of life are imbalanced. Some forces are just more important.
•	People who employ 80/20 thinking are good at achieving happiness.
•	Effective 80/20 thinkers are masters at prioritizing and delegating the rest.
•	Pick tasks with the highest reward that require the least effort.
•	Life-changing insight requires consistent, high-value thinking and reflection.
•	Solve problems by removing impediments. Like the World Wide Web did by removing distance or like fast food restaurants did by removing waiters.

Get to know the author.
Woody Acre
The following are some of his Accomplishments and Achievements

In the shadow of Red River, where the winds of Grand Forks, North Dakota, carried the bite of winter even in spring, Woody Acre was born on a snowy November morning in 1951. The son of Gertrude, a schoolteacher with a passion for literature, and Wise, a Bricklayer whose hands were calloused and thick but steady with skill, Woody grew up in a modest clapboard house on the city's west side.

The Acre's were not wealthy, but their home was rich with encouragement. Gertrude read to Woody from weathered copies of *The Odyssey* and *Huckleberry Finn*, while Thomas taught him to wield a wrench before he could ride a bike. These early influences shaped a boy who saw no boundary between mind and muscle. By the time Woody was eight, his wiry frame and boundless energy marked him as different. At school, he was restless, his mind racing faster than his teachers could keep up. Physical education was his sanctuary. In eighth grade, at thirteen, he discovered the rope climb—a test of strength, grit, and will. The gym at Central Junior High was a cavernous space its air thick with the scent of sweat and old varnish. Woody gripped the knotted rope, his palms burning, and hauled himself upward with a ferocity that stunned his classmates. When the stopwatch stopped, he had shattered the Minnesota state high-school record for the rope climb, a feat unheard of for a junior high student. The record, etched in the annals of Minnesota athletics, stood as a testament to his raw potential.

That same year, Woody's aquatic prowess emerged. The YMCA pool became his second home, its chlorinated waters a canvas for his ambition. He qualified for the senior high-school swim team, a rarity for an eighth-grader. Each morning, before the sun breached the horizon, Woody swam a mile—forty lengths of the 25-yard pool—his strokes rhythmic, his breath disciplined. His lung capacity was extraordinary; he could swim over one hundred yards underwater on a single breath, a skill honed through countless hours of practice. His coach, a gruff former Olympian named Coach Larson, saw in Woody a rare blend of talent and tenacity. "You're not just swimming," Larson told him. "You're fighting the water. Keep fighting."

At fourteen, inspired by a magazine article on wind-powered vehicles, Woody built a three-wheeled sail car. Scavenging a tricycle frame, a bed-rail from a junkyard, and the wheels from his old soapbox derby racer, he constructed a contraption that looked like a child's fever dream.

In an empty parking lot near the edge of town, with winds gusting, Woody sailed across the asphalt, the sail car wobbling but holding. His laughter echoed as he steered, a boy in love with creation and motion.

Woody's competitive spirit found its fullest expression in the pool. At fourteen, he set the junior-high-school record for the one-hundred-yard freestyle, clocking a time that left spectators speechless. The record, carved into the school's trophy case, stood unbroken for twenty-two years, a monument to his dominance.

By sixteen, Woody competed in the Junior Olympics, where he claimed two silver medals—one in the 100-meter freestyle, where he surged past competitors in the final lap, and another as the anchor in the 400-meter freestyle relay, his powerful strokes pulling his team from third to second. His bronze in the 400-meter individual medley relay was hard-fought, each stroke a battle against exhaustion. The medals hung on his bedroom wall, glinting in the moonlight as he dreamed of greater challenges.

But Woody's talents weren't confined to water. On the track, he ran the one-hundred-yard dash in the ten-second bracket, his lean legs a blur as he tore across the cinder oval. His versatility was matched by his ingenuity.

High school ended, but Woody's hunger for achievement did not. At nineteen, he started his first company, Acre Construction, a small outfit that took on odd jobs around. The city, with its boom-and-bust economy tied to shipping and industry, was a proving ground. Woody worked as a general laborer, hauling lumber and mixing concrete, but his ambition pushed him further. He learned stonemasonry, laying bricks with the precision of a surgeon.

As a rough carpenter, he framed houses under the relentless Minnesota sun; as a finish carpenter, he crafted cabinets with an artisan's touch. Roofing was his least favorite task—scrambling across slick shingles in rain or snow—

but he mastered it, his work ethic unyielding.

Woody's hands were tools of transformation. He built houses that sheltered families, apartment buildings that housed hundreds, churches with steeples piercing the sky, schools where children learned, and stores that buzzed with commerce. Each project was a canvas, each nail a brushstroke. By his mid-twenties, he owned three construction companies, employing dozens of workers across Minnesota and Wisconsin.

His leadership was instinctive: he knew when to crack a joke to lighten the mood and when to push his crew to meet a deadline.

Heavy equipment became an extension of his body. He operated cranes with the delicacy of a watchmaker, maneuvered front-end loaders through muddy sites, and dug trenches with backhoes. Bobcats and forklifts obeyed his command, and he drove eighteen-wheelers loaded with materials across state lines, the rumble of the engine a familiar comfort. But construction was only the beginning.

In a machine shop in Superior, Wisconsin, Woody discovered a new passion. He learned to operate lathes and mills, shaping metal with precision. Welding became second nature, the arc's blue glow illuminating his focus. He took on layout and design work, sketching small parts and complex assemblies, his pencil tracing lines that would become reality.

As head of a drafting department, he ordered supplies, scheduled projects, and interviewed candidates, his authority tempered by a genuine respect for his team. His colleagues nicknamed him "The General," not for his sternness but for his ability to rally people around a shared goal.

Woody's life was not all toil. The open road beckoned, and he answered with a Harley-Davidson he bought at twenty-one. Over a decade, he rode through all forty-eight contiguous states, the bike's roar his soundtrack.

The most devastating injury came at twenty-six, when he drove off a hundred thirty-foot cliff. In the accident he broke his neck in two places and tore the left side of his scalp off. The surgery to reattach it was grueling, the recovery months long.

He got arrested for getting into an argument with an unruly flight attendant, though it was no fault of his own. The airline gifted him tickets to Hawaii to make up for the trouble they caused.

In Hawaii, he rented a motorcycle and cruised along Maui's volcanic cliffs, the Pacific stretching endlessly to his left. He rode every paved highway on the island and stayed in a condo on the beach.

The road was freedom, but it was also peril. In Minnesota, a deer leapt onto the highway, and Woody's bike struck it at 60 miles an hour. He skidded across the pavement on the top of his head back and arms, his shirt torn to shreds, but walked away with only three broken ribs a collapsed lung and a ton of road rash. A story he tells with a wry grin.

Mountains were another obsession. Woody climbed three peaks over 14,000 plus feet—Pikes Peak 14,115 feet, 82 degrees at the base in Manitou Springs it was 27 degree at the summit, Mount Evans 14,265 feet, and Mount Elbert 14,439 feet the highest summit in elevation in the Rocky Mountains of north America the only mountain taller in the contiguous United States is Mount Whitney at 14.505 feet—each ascent a solitary pilgrimage.

On Evans, at 13,500 feet, a blizzard trapped him. The wind howled, visibility dropped to zero, and the cold seeped into his bones. After his lean to blew away in eighty mile an hour winds he found himself huddled behind a cotoneaster shrub, covered in a snow drift. Woody rationed his energy bars and waited out the storm, his mind sharp despite the fear. When the skies cleared, he summited, the world below a patchwork of green and gray.

In Minnesota's Boundary Waters Canoe Area, Woody hiked the Sioux-Hustler Trail, a 32-mile loop through dense forest and rocky lakeshores. One evening, as he cooked over a small fire, a black bear charged from the underbrush. Woody grabbed his metal water bottle and banged it against a rock, the clang echoing through the trees. The bear hesitated, then retreated, leaving Woody's heart pounding but his resolve intact.

The sea was his final frontier. In the Trans-Superior International Yacht Race, Woody was first mate in Class-C sloop through Lake Superior's treacherous waves. His crew, a mix of seasoned sailors and eager novices, trusted his instincts as he navigated squalls and shifting winds to claim victory.

48 Foot Morgan Center Cockpit

Years later, he sailed the Florida Keys in a forty-eight-foot Morgan, anchoring near coral reefs to dive into turquoise waters. The sea, like the mountains and the road, was a place where Woody felt alive.

Woody's mind was as restless as his body. As a mechanical engineer, he thrived on solving problems others deemed impossible. He remembers what his grandpa told him; "if it's difficult, we'll have it done right away. If it's impossible, it will take a while longer."

In a manufacturing plant in Minneapolis, he worked as a manufacturing engineer, streamlining production lines and cutting costs. His innovations led to several patents— designs for machinery and components that improved efficiency and safety.

As a mechanical engineering manager, he led teams on multimillion-dollar projects, from designing industrial equipment to retrofitting factories. He designed solutions for such companies as; 3M, Allen Bradley, Amana, BASF, Caterpillar, Delphi, Dixie-Narco Electrolux, Frigidaire Home Products, General Electric, Honeywell, John Deer, Larson/Glastron Boats Inc., Masonite International, Maytag, Mercedes Benz, Rockwell International, Seagate, Vendo, W. C. Wood, just to name a few.

His ability to bridge technical detail with big-picture strategy made him invaluable.

Woody owned an engineering firm, Acre Solutions, where he implemented and taught Material Requirements Planning (MRP), Capacity Requirements Planning (CRP), and Enterprise Resource Planning (ERP) systems. These systems transformed chaotic workflows into models of efficiency, earning him a reputation as a visionary.

He led sales teams to millions in revenue, his charisma closing deals with clients ranging from local startups to Fortune 500 companies.

For several years, Woody owned a recording studio in St. Cloud, a passion project that blended his technical skills with a love for music. He recorded local bands, tweaking soundboards to capture raw emotion, his engineer's precision enhancing every track.

As CEO of a multimillion-dollar manufacturing corporation for over twelve years, Woody reached the pinnacle of his professional life. He navigated boardroom politics with the same ease he brought to construction

sites, his decisions shaping the company's future.

Woody's triumphs were matched by trials that would have broken lesser men. In his twenties, he fell into the grip of drug and alcohol addiction, a dark period fueled by the pressures of his burgeoning career.

The battle was brutal, but Woody emerged sober, his will forged anew. His body, however, bore the scars of a life lived fearlessly. He broke his ribs four times—twice in construction accidents, once in a motorcycle accident, and once in a fall while climbing.

His skull was fractured three times: a beating with a baseball, a car accident at twenty-six, and a fall from a deck eight feet onto the concrete landing on his head.

A collapsed lung followed a motorcycle crash, and a burst appendix nearly killed him at ten years old, the surgery leaving a jagged scar across his abdomen.

One childhood accident was particularly harrowing: an arrow, fired by a friend during a game of archery, pierced his right eye, and he was one of the first in Minnesota to receive dissolving sutures that saved his vision. Woody adapted; his resilience unshaken.

He sewed up a knife wound himself after a barroom scuffle, using a sewing kit and a mirror, his hands steady despite the pain.

A metal shard pierced his hand on a construction site, requiring surgery. He was beaten with a baseball bat in

another altercation, his ribs cracking
under the blows.

A stabbing in his thirties left a scar
on his rib cage, fluid drained from his
lungs Thoracentesis twice and
Paracentesis three times.

Three knee surgeries followed
years of physical strain, and a broken
neck from driving off a cliff so he had to
wear a halo brace that was screwed into

his head. Yet Woody endured, each
scar a badge of survival.

By his fifties, Woody could have
retired, his wealth and reputation
secure. Instead, he chose to give back.
He wrote several books— *You Know
What I Hate*, a memoir of what he

learned during his engineering career; 19 books of *TALES*, a collection of short stories; and *Merit* a guide to leadership and resilience. Each book was a labor of love, blending practical advice with vivid storytelling.

His speaking engagements were legendary. At colleges, clubs, and corporations, Woody delivered presentations on sales, management, engineering, and organizational strategy. His talks were performances, weaving humor, hardship, and insight into narratives that left audiences inspired.

He recounted surviving the bear attack, summiting mountains, and leading multimillion-dollar deals, but his message was universal: perseverance turns dreams into reality.

Now in his sixties, Woody Acre remains a force of nature. His hair is gray, his body scarred, but his spirit is unbroken. He lives in a cabin outside a larger town, where he writes, consults, and occasionally rides his restored motorcycles.

His life is a testament to the power of versatility—of mastering the pool, the road, the sea, the boardroom, and the wilderness.

Woody's story is not one of invincibility but of endurance. From the boy who broke records to the man who built empires, from the adventurer who faced bears and blizzards to the leader who inspired thousands,

His legacy is not just in the buildings he constructed or the patents he filed but, in the lives, he touched, the lessons he shared, and the unyielding belief that no challenge is too great.

Very successful people said these things.

Valuable Quotes

1.   "There will be obstacles. There will be doubters. There will be mistakes. But with hard work, there are no limits."
        -   Michael Phelps.

2.   "If you're going through hell, keep going."
        -   Winston Churchill.

3.   "Rock bottom became the solid foundation in which I built my life."
        -   J. K. Rowling.

4.   "Obstacles are those frightful things you see when you take your eyes off your goals."
        -   Henry Ford.

5.   "He who sweats more in training bleeds less in war."
        -   Greek proverb.

6.   "Failure is the condiment that gives success its flavor."

-       *Truman Capote.*

7.   *"When you meet obstacles with gratitude, your perception starts to shift, <u>resistance </u>loses its power, and grace finds a home within you."*
-       *Oprah Winfrey.*

8.   *"We are what we repeatedly do. Excellence, then, is not an act, but a habit."*
-       *Aristotle.*

9.   *"You win not by chance but by preparation."*
-       *Roger Maris.*

10.   *"I am thankful for all of those who said no to me. It's because of them I'm doing it myself."*
-       *Albert Einstein.*

11.   *"It is better to anticipate than to react."*
-       *Bob Knight.*

12.   *"Some men see things as they are and say why. I dream things that never were and say why not."*

-	Bobby Kennedy.

13.	"Don't be distracted by criticism. Remember - the only taste of success some people have is when they take a bite out of you."
-	Zig Ziglar.

14.	"The future rewards those who press on. I don't have time to feel sorry for myself. I don't have time to complain. I'm going to press on."
-	Barack Obama.

15.	"It's not that I'm so smart, it's just that I stay with problems longer."
-	Albert Einstein.

16.	"In matters of style, swim with the current; in matters of principle, stand like a rock."
-	Thomas Jefferson.

17.	"The best wisdom comes from the hardest struggle."
-	Xavier Rudd.

18.   'If you always do
what you've always done, you'll always
get what you've always got."
    -    Henry Ford

19.   "**Insanity** is doing the same thing
over and over and expecting different
results."
    -    Albert Einstein

20.   Here are 50 quotes to inspire you
to <u>succeed in the face of failures</u>,
setbacks, and barriers.

21.   "Success is not final; failure is not
fatal: It is the courage to continue that
counts."
    -    Winston S. Churchill

22.   "It is better to fail in originality than
to succeed in imitation."
    -    Herman Melville

23.   "The road to success and the road
to failure are almost exactly the same."
    -    Colin R. Davis

24.   *"Success usually comes to those who are too busy to be looking for it."*
-        *Henry David Thoreau*

25.   *"Opportunities don't happen. You create them."*
-        *Chris Grosser*

26.   *"Don't be afraid to give up the good to go for the great."*
27.   *--John D. Rockefeller*

28.   *"I find that the harder I work, the more luck I seem to have."*
-        *Thomas Jefferson*

29.   *"There are two types of people who will tell you that you cannot make a difference in this world: those who are afraid to try and those who are afraid you will succeed."*
-        *Ray Goforth*

30.   *"Successful people do what unsuccessful people are not willing to do. Don't wish it were easier; wish you were better."*
-        *Jim Rohn*

31.   "Try not to become a man of success. Rather become a man of value."
-       Albert Einstein

32.   "Never give in except to convictions of honor and good sense."
-       Winston Churchill

33.   "Stop chasing the money and start chasing the passion."
-       Tony Hsieh

34.   "Success is walking from failure to failure with no loss of enthusiasm."
-       Winston Churchill

35.   "I owe my success to having listened respectfully to the very best advice, and then going away and doing the exact opposite."
-       G. K. Chesterton

36.   "Would you like me to give you a formula for success? It's quite simple, really: Double your rate of failure. You are thinking of failure as the enemy of success. But it isn't at all. You can be discouraged by failure or you can learn

from it, so go ahead and make mistakes. Make all you can. Because remember that's where you will find success."

*-		Thomas J. Watson*

*37.	"If you are not willing to risk the usual, you will have to settle for the ordinary."*

*-		-Jim Rohn*

*38.	"The ones who are crazy enough to think they can change the world, are the ones that do."*

*-		Anonymous*

*39.	"Do one thing every day that scares you."*

*-		Anonymous*

*40.	"All progress takes place outside the comfort zone."*

*-		Michael John Bobak*

*41.	"People who succeed have momentum. The more they succeed, the more they want to succeed, and the more they find a way to succeed. Similarly, when someone is failing, the*

tendency is to get on a downward spiral that can even become a self-fulfilling prophecy."
- *Tony Robbins*

42. "Don't let the fear of losing be greater than the excitement of winning."
- *Robert Kiyosaki*

43. "If you really look closely, most overnight successes took a long time."
- *Steve Jobs*

44. "The real test is not whether you avoid this failure, because you won't. It's whether you let it harden or shame you into inaction, or whether you learn from it; whether you choose to persevere."
- *Barack Obama*

45. "The only limit to our realization of tomorrow will be our doubts of today."
- *Franklin D. Roosevelt*

46. "Character cannot be developed in ease and quiet. Only through experience of trial and suffering can the soul be strengthened, ambition inspired, and success achieved."

-        *Helen Keller*

47.   *"The way to get started is to quit talking and begin doing."*
-        *Walt Disney*

48.   *"The successful warrior is the average man, with laser-like focus."*
-        *Bruce Lee*

49.   *"There are no secrets to success. It is the result of preparation, hard work, and learning from failure."*
-        *Colin Powell*

50.   *"Success seems to be connected with action. Successful people keep moving. They make mistakes, but they don't quit."*
-        *Conrad Hilton*

51.   *"If you really want to do something, you'll find a way. If you don't, you'll find an excuse."*
-        *Jim Rohn*

52.   *"I cannot give you the formula for success, but I can give you the formula*

for failure--It is: Try to please
everybody."
-   Herbert Bayard Swope

53.   "Success isn't just about what you
accomplish in your life; it's about what
you inspire others to do."
-   Unknown

54.   "Fall seven times and stand up
eight."
-   Japanese Proverb

55.   "Some people dream of success
while others wake up and work."
-   Unknown

56.   "If you can dream it, you can do
it."
-   Walt Disney

57.   "The difference between who you
are and who you want to be is what you
do."
-   Unknown

58. "A successful man is one who can lay a firm foundation with the bricks that other throw at him."
    -    *David Brinkley*

59. "In order to succeed, your desire for success should be greater than your fear of failure."
    -    *Bill Cosby*

60. "In order to succeed, we must first believe that we can."
    -    *Nikos Kazantzakis*

61. "Many of life's failures are people who did not realize how close they were to success when they gave up."
    -    *Thomas Edison*

62. "Don't be distracted by criticism. Remember--the only taste of success some people get is to take a bite out of you."
    -    *Zig Ziglar*

63. "The secret of success is to do the common thing uncommonly well."
    -    *John D. Rockefeller Jr.*

64.   *"You know you are on the road to success if you would do your job, and not be paid for it."*
-    Oprah Winfrey

65.   *"There is a powerful driving force inside every human being that, once unleashed, can make any vision, dream, or desire a reality."*
-    Anthony Robbins

66.   *"The secret to success is to know something nobody else knows."*
-    Aristotle Onassis

67.   *"I failed my way to success."*
-    Thomas Edison

68.   *"I never did anything worth doing by accident, nor did any of my inventions come indirectly through accident, except the phonograph. No, when I have fully decided that a result is worth getting, I go about it, and make trial after trial, until it comes."*
-    Thomas Edison

69.   *"The only place where success comes before work is in the dictionary."*
-   Vidal Sassoon

70.   *"Keep on going, and the chances are that you will stumble on something, perhaps when you are least expecting it. I never heard of anyone ever stumbling on something sitting down."*
-   Charles F. Kettering

It might be interesting; I suggest looking up and reading about the people that made these quotes.

Notes: Use the next few pages to write down area's that you may want to improve. Identify helpful page numbers for references.